WHY I WRITE

Why I Write

Thoughts on the Craft of Fiction

EDITED BY

WILL BLYTHE

LITTLE, BROWN AND COMPANY
Boston   New York   Toronto   London

FIRST EDITION

Joy Williams's essay, Barry Hannah's essay, and Mark Richard's story
first appeared in *The Oxford American*
David Foster Wallace's essay and Amy Hempel's essay
first appeared in *Fiction Writer*
Richard Ford's essay first appeared in *Granta*

LIBRARY OF CONGRESS CATALOGING-IN-PUBLICATION DATA
Why I write : thoughts on the craft of fiction /
edited by Will Blythe. — 1st ed.
p. cm.
Twenty-six original essays on writing.
ISBN 0-316-10229-6
1. Authorship. 2. Fiction — Authorship. I. Blythe, Will.
PN165.W485 1988
808'.02 — dc21 98-21419

10 9 8 7 6 5 4 3 2 1

MV—NY

Published simultaneously in Canada by
Little, Brown & Company (Canada) Limited

Printed in the United States of America

IN HONOR OF

LeGette Blythe
Esther Blythe
Anna Nassif
David Nassif

Contents

‿⟋

ACKNOWLEDGMENTS

The editor would like to thank Michael Pietsch and Amanda Murray for, among other qualities, their patience. Thanks also to the writers whose work makes up this book.

Introduction

WILL BLYTHE

From sea to shining sea, in bookstores and homes, and even in those Swiss chalet–style condos dotting the purple-mountained majesties, the shelves of America are groaning under the weight of "how-to-write" books. These sprightly, optimistic manuals suggest some odd, unspoken consensus that imaginative writing is an activity well worth pursuing for us Americans, perhaps as a kind of graphomaniacal self-therapy. Evidently, it's no longer enough to read stories; we must write them as well. Everybody in the pool! But given that we all seem to want to know *how* to write, shouldn't we first take a step backward, away from the water's edge, and ask the big question lurking furtively behind the *how*, which is *why* even attempt to write literature in the first place? Why, oh why? That's what this book is about.

Unquestionably, there are many compelling reasons *not* to write. Some are mundane, like having a job, a spouse, a headache. These things can take time and energy away from the creation of literature. So can not having a job, a spouse, and a headache. (In regard to the absence of headache, it must be said that you *can* feel too *good* to write.) There are other mighty rationales for shirking the pen. Not enough money. Too little experience. Bad speller. Not good enough yet. Not good enough compared to García Márquez. Not good enough compared to Shakespeare. Better than Shakespeare but no one seems to agree. Too much ambition. Insufficient ambition. Paranoia. Alcohol. Heroin. Gas pains. Gout. Hay fever.

And of course, there are always powerful metaphysical reasons for not writing. For instance, deep existential dread. The distortions of solitude. The ravages of time. Black holes. The eventual death of the solar system. Being adrift in a meaningless universe in which everything is floating away from everything else. The temptation of silence. By this, I mean that sometimes silence seems more articulate, more full of possibility than language itself; it is the realm of the vision, of the masterfully unwritten, of astounding books that will forever be undiminished by their narrowing in reality.

Wait, there's more. Back here in the brawling American marketplace, it's easy to feel that this is a society in which literature all too often gets shoved behind the traffic barricades by the beefy cops of hype while the clamorous parade of mass culture goose-steps triumphantly down the avenue. "Get over to the cultural margins, you losers," the police yell, vexed by such unglamorous duties. As Don DeLillo has said of his fellow novelists, "We're one beat away from becoming elevator music."

Plus — and I think this is widely known — a writer with a capacity for composing novels and short stories can usually make more money slaving away for the movies and TV. So, really, why does anyone write fiction?

*   *   *

This is evidently a question that has been occurring to people (mainly writers) for quite some time, and for good reason, it seems. I remember the first moment it occurred to me, way back in the balmy spring of 1968. I was soldiering through the fifth grade at Glenwood Elementary School in Chapel Hill, North Carolina. One sunny afternoon in Miss Farrior's reading class, in between casting frequent and admiring glances at my new desert boots and sending the same sort of looks over my shoulder toward the lovely Patty Midgette and Mitzi Cherry, I came across an article in my *Weekly Reader* about the mortality rates of various professions (in retrospect, this study seems altogether too wonderfully morbid for the *Weekly Reader* — might it have actually appeared in that brutal, unsparing *Scholastic* magazine?). Right *down* there with lumberjacks and stock-car drivers in terms of suffering early death were professional writers. Now, I could understand buying the farm by chopping down a tree on top of yourself, or by spinning into a concrete wall at 165 miles an hour. Death loves the woods and the racetrack. But what precisely were the risk factors associated with sitting quietly at a desk, scribbling onto a sheet of paper?

Those statistics seemed inconceivable to me at the time (sadly, a little less so now) because my grandfather LeGette Blythe was a writer, and he was one of the happiest people I've ever known. I'm not talking about spritzy, bubbly, lick-your-face happiness; no, I mean the deep, underground-river kind that makes a person steady and content and a boon to his fellows. Unless you are family or from a certain generation of North Carolina readers, mostly died out now, you probably haven't heard of my grandfather. He was born in 1900 in the tiny town of Huntersville, North Carolina. As a child, he won a pair of shoes in an essay contest sponsored by the Mecklenburg County Fair. I always thought it was his first pair of shoes, but I'm now told that it wasn't; it wouldn't have been unlike my grandfather, honest though he was, to embellish a story ever so slightly. (There are a few overly literal-minded members of my family who say I've inherited this tendency from him.)

He eventually became a newspaperman in Charlotte, famous among his peers for not taking notes and not playing poker. He published several books while still a reporter, including one novel, *Bold Galilean*, that became a best-seller for the University of North Carolina Press. When the editors of the *Charlotte Observer* wouldn't give him a leave of absence to write a new novel, banking on their suspicion that he couldn't afford to give up employment, he called their bluff and quit. He was fifty years old, with a wife, three children, and bills to pay. Over the next four decades, he paid those bills, turning out plays, biographies, history, and fiction (including several biblical novels), some twenty-nine works in all.

The citizens of the Bible were as real to him as his family and neighbors. The story is often told in my family of how he once drove up to the edge of Lake Norman, where he was mistaken for a game warden by several locals who were fishing without the benefit of a license. "How y'all doing?" he said. "Catching anything?" "No sir, no sir," they insisted, pretending to be unaware of the poles bobbing in front of them. (In truth, no one could have been further from a game warden. My grandfather's sympathies tended entirely toward the underdog. He evinced a mild truculence toward improperly or heavily asserted authority, having as a young reporter been bashed into unconsciousness by a hired thug outside a textile mill in Gastonia during the strike of 1929.)

The fishermen relaxed that day by the lake only when my grandfather, apparently oblivious to the discomforting effect he was having, began telling them how Lake Norman was the exact size of the Sea of Galilee, and how the location of the grand town of Cornelius corresponded precisely to that of the Judean city of Capernaum. "Is that right?" the fishermen said, sensing that this might indeed be a day of deliverance, not to mention free fish. It wasn't so much that Pappy, as we called him, saw the Holy Land superimposed on the local map in a kind of geographical allegory. Instead, Mecklenburg County *was* the Holy Land. Who needed Jerusalem when you had Caldwell Station? Over the years, he defied every chance he had to actually visit the dry landscape of his waking dreams. If you were openhearted and sympathetic, history was here now. For my grandfather, it was a mere quirk of chronology that Paul and Judas (the subjects of two of his novels) were not there beside him on the clay banks of Lake Norman, admiring the view.

For as much as the world-at-large intrigued him, no part of it fascinated him more than his home, Mecklenburg County, in western North Carolina. He lived just a hundred yards or so away from the house he had been born in. He knew the night skies, the vegetation, the fields, the creek beds, the old homesteads, even the cats that lived (because he fed them) in the woods behind the house. He knew the citizens of Huntersville as if they were kin, and if you *were* kin . . . well, either way you had better be prepared to talk for a while when you saw him coming. Many was the noontime when my grandmother had to drag him away from the informal gatherings on the lawn after church. "Come on, Gette," she'd bark, being made of sterner stuff than he. It was a hopeless task. He could ask you questions until your head spun, as my father's frequently did when he tried to explain to Pappy some obscure point about sodium transfer in the kidneys. Pappy liked to keep abreast of things. Some days late in his life, he would stand at the window of the house he built for his family in 1928, counting the cars that rolled by on the highway. This wasn't some senile arithmetical mania so much as another way of proudly determining how much his hometown had grown. He had never acquired the antidevelopment bias that is understandably rampant late in this century. He would return from one of his walks shaking his head in delighted, open-eyed wonder at the establishment of a Dairy Queen in some old, kudzu-ridden pasture.

Although he always made himself available to his seven grandchildren, being forever willing to take us out to the garden or bend our ears with family history, he wrote very hard until near the end of his life. He kept deadlines, his own and others', disappearing into his cluttered study (books, old shoes, a reel-to-reel tape recorder, a hornet's nest) for a few hours almost every day, when we heard his typewriter clattering as he pecked away with two fingers, like the old-fashioned reporter he had been. In the closet of his study, he brewed homemade wine that occasionally detonated when the fermentation became too extravagant for its container. There was also, I think, an extra bit of fermentation, of vim, of force, in my grandfather when he wrote — a kind of bottled intensity that ended up on the page. Photographs of him at the typewriter reveal Pappy in a light we rarely witnessed at close range — lost to us, to the world, deep in concentration, utterly elsewhere. And yet he made the process of composition sound maddeningly simple. I once asked him how he wrote his books. "Well," he said, "if you know the beginning of your story, and you know the end, all you have to do is get from one to the other."

For Pappy, writing was part and parcel with the rest of his life, not an extreme quest requiring a hermit's hut in the desert. No, several hours a day upstairs in that maze of a study would do. He was no literary naïf: he wanted to make money, as his deal-making letters to agents and editors confirm, sometimes poignantly. And he was aware that he wasn't exactly famous in the way of, say, F. Scott Fitzgerald. I remember his reading *The Great Gatsby* at the beach one summer. After he finished, he pronounced it a "pretty fine book," which was high praise since he was not a florid man. "I guess he did pretty good, didn't he?" my grandfather said of Fitzgerald. "But I don't believe he had a happier life than I've had. No, I don't think I would trade with him." He died on Halloween afternoon, 1993. He had asked my grandmother if his dying would be all right with her. She probably told him to hush.

Why did he write? His life is emblematic of fiction writers in that he wrote, in part, because he was good at it. He got paid for it (not an insubstantial thing); he made a name for himself with it. And as with other fiction writers, making stories put him in contact with otherwise inaccessible regions, in his case, the Holy Land. I also think that writing was his gift, as it is the gift of the authors who have contributed to this book, and that a gift avoided and unexercised is deep trouble indeed. My grandfather would surely have seen the Old Testament story of the talents applying here. He located his motivation somewhere between the customs of a trade and the dictates of compulsion. Not every novelist dives deep under the ocean of existence, nor does every one wield an ax with which to strike the frozen sea within. Would my grandfather have been a better writer if he'd been an unhappier man? Perhaps, though unhappiness takes its toll, and what it offers in the way of insight, it can take away in energy and conviction. Anyway, he had his sadnesses and disappointments, mind you, and he felt the pain of many beyond himself. It's not as if any of us escapes sorrow for long. My grandfather's virtues were not exactly simple. Goodness never is.

*   *   *

As with the heart and most criminal defendants, writers always have their reasons.

There are, actually, dozens of reasons, as the following essays attest. And that's the way it's been through the ages, apparently: a myriad of private compulsions, a welter of incontestable desires. In his midtwenties, Franz Kafka, insurance man, remarked, "God doesn't want me to write, but I must write." E. M. Cioran proposed that "a book is a postponed suicide." Jorge Luis Borges scribbled to "ease the passing of time."

Other writers betray evidence of a bloody psychic shootout between misanthropy and altruism. William Gass creates literature, he says, "because I hate. A lot. Hard." He also asserts that the "aim of the artist ought to be to bring into the world objects which do not already exist there, and objects which are especially worthy of love." Samuel Johnson famously proclaimed that "no man but a blockhead ever wrote except for money." (Mark Jacobson, in his apologia on page 116, asserts the same.) But Johnson also declared that the "only end of writing is to enable readers to better enjoy life or better . . . endure it."

These are large, compassionate sentiments, their enormity the province of philosophers, who are willing to make the sort of grand pronouncements about art that most fiction writers shy away from. The latter's capacities are more often for the specific at the expense of the general, for the exception rather than the rule; they are well aware of the psychological burdens that come with grandiosity, with overclaiming for one's work. In fact, let's allow a philosopher, the Spaniard Ortega y Gasset, to step in where fiction writers fear to tread. "The possibility of constructing human souls," he wrote, "is perhaps the major asset of future novelists."

Now, constructing human souls is a pretty big responsibility. In fact, it used to be God's job. If writers had to think of salvation every time they sat down to type . . . well, they might as well be preachers. It's not that literature doesn't save souls; I suspect it has a better record in that department than the church. But God help the writer who pulls up to his desk with soul-saving in mind. Not that many American writers could acknowledge such an impetus for their own work, so great is their inherent modesty or their inherent fear of seeming immodest.

That said, I'm convinced that writers, in spite of themselves, do preserve souls, even make them. It's a little embarrassing to say this, because I'm not even sure I really believe in the soul — not, at least, in the spooky little ghost-aura that goes with us like a shadow, that might, like a parasite abandoning a dead host, fly out of us when we die. By soul, I mean a certain depth, an inwardness, a watchfulness. Detachment, solitude, stillness.

You might find it in a man sitting in his backyard on a summer night, clinking the ice in his gin and tonic. Staring into the window of his own house, watching his wife watch the Atlanta Braves on the Superstation. He's trying to remember exactly what passionate love feels like, the difference between eternity and boredom.

You might encounter it in a securities lawyer. She is supposed to be working this weekend but instead stares moonily out the window at the Woolworth Building, thinking to herself how peculiar it is to be alive at four o'clock on a Saturday afternoon. Just strange. She can't quite get over the oddness of it all.

You'd also be likely to discover soul in someone quietly reading. I can almost guarantee it. And indeed, the corollary to the question of why one writes is the question of why one reads. Among the functions of literature in general, and of fiction in particular, is the way they sharpen the ear and open the heart. The poet Joseph Brodsky once suggested, not altogether in jest, that the world's leaders might be better chosen for their views on Dickens and Stendhal and Cervantes rather than for their analyses of foreign policy and domestic affairs.

The very act of reading literature, the anticommunalism of it, the slow drift into reverie, the immersion into the charismatic black-and-white grids of the page — all of this emphatically unplugs us from that other grid, that beeping, noisome electronic grid that attempts to snare us in a web of reflex, of twitch and spasm. Does this make the pursuit of literature a Luddite maneuver, with all of the shadowings of melancholy and futility attendant on such rebellions? I suspect that to the contrary, passionate reading will become a form of permanent opposition, as vigorous and rooted and abiding as the great religious movements that we have seen rekindled in the last few decades. It often strikes me that one of the few moves left for the literary avant-garde (which is looking plain tuckered out these days — it's been a busy century) would be to plant a woody glade, dense with bamboo and shade and silence, in the midst of the roaring city of news and corporate blather, away from the tiring intimations of hipness trotted out by tireless marketeers. Anybody who's ever danced to rock 'n' roll knows how much fun mass-cult. can be, but it's getting increasingly difficult to forget how uniform are its tastes, how deadly is its ubiquity, and how ugly it is in its monotony.

In the spirit of my grandfather, then, this book is about the happiness of writing, about writing as an antidote to boredom and monotony and uniformity. It tells you from a variety of points of view — some acerbic, some rhapsodic, some as straightforward as a recipe — why writing (and its common-law husband, reading) are worth doing, why they're absolutely fun and pleasurable (except when they're not) and essential, whether you're Fitzgerald, or whether you're just you.

A few final notes. Why, to begin with, did I select twenty-six *fiction* writers, as opposed to poets or journalists, for this collection? Simple. I'm partial to the form. More often than not, fiction, with its beautiful deceptions and its artful lies, reveals far more than fact ever will. We breathe in air, we exhale stories: who we saw on our way to the laundromat, why we didn't get in until six in the morning, how we fell in love with a voice that came in the window off a darkened street. In this sense, we—all of us—every day, in one way or another, write fiction.

Nonfiction, by contrast, still strikes me as a slightly less exalted genre (though, as always, the question is not so much *what* a piece of writing is as whether it's any good). To the extent that journalists over the last thirty-five years or so have asserted a greater claim to making literature — and I think they have — it's largely due to their having borrowed the techniques and license of novelists and short-story writers. In the interest of their work, these nonfiction writers have had to submit to the philosophical proposition that reality is largely created by the observer, which makes it an awful lot like, well, fiction.

As for poetry (and its practitioners' exclusion from these pages): call me a rube or a philistine, but I, for one, have never felt that the rhythms of fiction, its buried music, are one lick less glorious than those of poetry. In fact, I suspect that the elements of sound and meter that go into making a compelling fictional voice are, partly because they're not foregrounded, trickier to deploy in prose than in verse. Stories must not only advance through time (which a poem need not do), they must also sound right. Prose, too, lives and dies by the beat.

Now, I don't want to start a sectarian feud here. I like poetry and even a couple of poets. And these days, poets have a tougher row to hoe than fiction writers — not too many people want to buy the effete little vegetables they're raising in those lonely gardens. No, poetry's fine. It's just that for far too long, fiction, with its greater proximity to ordinary speech, has gotten a bum rap for being a more primitive form of language. No sir, I just can't take it anymore, watching poetry climbing solo up Mount Olympus to the evolutionary peak of language, with fiction the faithful Sherpa trudging far behind, lugging the tent and the cookstove and the freeze-dried goodies and the satin pillows to make poetry cumfy through the icy night.

Clearly, then, this is an anthology dedicated to the partisan notion that writing fiction is — I won't say this too loudly, because some writers may feel I'll jinx things by admitting it — a form of happiness, of supreme awareness that, once experienced, can be given up only with the greatest reluctance. In the end, reading the wonderfully varied essays in *Why I Write* will be worth your while, particularly if you are a student of writing, because the book is a lodestone, a talisman, a collection of spells, the most obstreperous and cranky magic manual you will ever read. It places you in the accident-prone midst of the creative process, with all of its flukes and capriciousness, and yes, its occasional grandeur. *Why I Write* is an act of literary cosmology — twenty-six superb writers working their way back to the Big Bang of narrative fiction, trying to get at origins that can never, fortunately, be precisely traced. It's the story of their stories, where their fiction came from (to the extent that anyone can really say; remember, this is magic we are talking about), where it goes. The accounts here evoke the strange miracle — and miracle is not too strong a word — through which fiction is conjured into being.

When you read these essays, you will realize that there is no Interstate running directly from the writer's imagination to a finished piece of fiction. And if that seems a little daunting to those who like their road maps emblazoned with the most efficient route by Triple A, it's also a liberation. Forget the how-to manuals; assembled within this book are the real methods, the genuine genealogies of creation: this is the real story of writing. Writers can get where they're going by just about any route — overland, underground, through the air, in their dreams. The way is open.

Why I Write

At the Point of My Pen

NORMAN MAILER

I MAY NOT TELL YOU why I write — it could be too complicated for my mind — but I can tell you about my dear friend, my
oldest friend, Jean Malaquais, and why he writes.

I remember how it was with him forty years ago when he was in
his midforties and was working on a novel, *The Joker*. He would
spend fourteen hours a day at his desk. Since he was punctilious
about literary virtue to the point of vice, he would, what with dele-
tions, corrections, and revisions, manage to advance his narrative
two or three hundred words. One page a day for fourteen hours of
horrendous labor. Since his powers of concentration were intense, it was, indeed, a labor for which no other adjective applied.
Fourteen hours. Horrendous. I, a more self-indulgent writer, used
to complain that a thousand words in three or four hours was
hardly a fair bargain for me.

I asked him once, "Why do you insist on remaining a writer?
With your intelligence, with your culture, you could be success-

ful at so many things. Writing may not be a normal activity for you."

He happened to agree. "You are absolutely right," he said. "I am not a natural writer. There are even times when I detest this torture. I achieve so little of my aims."

His aims, needless to say, were immense. They were exactly at the center of the problem. "All right," I said, "why not do something else?"

"Never," he said.

"Never? Tell me why."

"The only time I know the truth is when it reveals itself at the point of my pen."

I have been thinking of Jean Malaquais's answer for forty years. I could go on at length about how I write to convey my anger at all that I think is wrong in this world, or I could speak of the mystery of the novelist's aesthetic — ah, to be able to create a world that exists on the terms one has given it! — or I could even, unlike Jean Malaquais, be able to say, "When it's a matter of making a living, you can't beat the hours." But finally, I subscribe to his reply. For me, it has the advantage of being incontestably true. The only time, right or wrong, that I feel a quintessential religious emotion — that the power of the truth is in me — comes on occasion when I write, no, even better: the only time I know the truth is at the point of my pen.

Uncanny the Singing That Comes from Certain Husks

JOY WILLIAMS

⟋

It's become fashionable these days to say that the writer writes because he is not whole: he has a wound, he writes to heal it. But who cares if the writer is not whole? Of course the writer is not whole, or even particularly well. There's something unwholesome and self-destructive about the entire writing process. Writers are like eremites or anchorites — natural-born eremites or anchorites — who seem puzzled as to why they went up the pole or into the cave in the first place. Why am I so isolate in this strange place? Why is my sweat being sold as elixir? And how have I become so enmeshed with words, mere words, phantoms?

Writers when they're writing live in a spooky, clamorous silence, a state somewhat like the advanced stages of prayer but without prayer's calming benefits. A writer turns his back on the day and the night and its large and little beauties, and tries, like some half-witted demiurge, to fashion other days and nights with words. It's absurd. Oh, it's silly, dangerous work indeed.

A writer starts out, I think, wanting to be a transfiguring agent, and ends up usually just making contact, contact with other human beings. This, unsurprisingly, is not enough. (Making contact with the self — healing the wound — is even less satisfactory.) Writers end up writing stories — or rather, stories' shadows — and they're grateful if they can, but it is not enough. Nothing the writer can do is ever enough.

E. M. Forster once told his friend Laurens van der Post that he could not finish a story that he had begun with great promise, even brilliance, because he did not like the way it would have to finish. Van der Post wrote, "The remark for me proved both how natural stories were to him and how acute was his sense of their significance, but at the same time revealed that his awareness was inadequate for the task the story imposed upon it."

I like van der Post's conception of story — as a stern taskmaster that demands the ultimate in awareness, that indeed *is* awareness. The significant story possesses more awareness than the writer writing it. The significant story is always greater than the writer writing it. This is the absurdity, the disorienting truth, the question that is not even a question, this is the koan of writing.

Malcolm Muggeridge wrote in an essay on Jesus, "When a person loses the isolation, the separateness which awareness of the presence of God alone can give, he becomes irretrievably part of a collectivity with only mass communications to shape its hopes, formulate its values and arrange its thinking."

Without the awareness of separateness, one can never be part of the whole, the nothingness that is God. This is the divine absurdity, the koan of faith.

Jean Rhys said that when she was a child she thought that God was a big book. I don't know what she thought when she was no longer a child. She probably wished that she could think of a big book as being God.

A writer's awareness must never be inadequate. Still, it will never be adequate to the greater awareness of the work itself, the work that the writer is trying to write. The writer must not really know what he is knowing, what he is learning to know when he writes, which is more than the knowing of it. A writer loves the dark, loves it, but is always fumbling around in the light. The writer is separate from his work but that's all the writer is — what he writes. A writer must be smart but not too smart. He must be dumb enough to break himself to harness. He must be reckless and patient and daring and dull — for what is duller than writing, trying to write? And he must never care — caring spoils everything. It compromises the work. It shows the writer's hand. The writer is permitted, even expected, to have compassion for his characters, but what are characters? Nothing but mystic symbols, magical emblems, ghosts of the writer's imagination.

The writer doesn't want to disclose or instruct or advocate, he wants to transmute and disturb. He cherishes the mystery, he cares for it like a fugitive in his cabin, his cave. He doesn't want to talk it into giving itself up. He would never turn it in to the authorities, the mass mind. The writer is somewhat of a fugitive himself, actually. He wants to escape his time, the obligations of his time, and, by writing, transcend them. The writer does not like to follow orders, not even the orders of his own organizing intellect. The moment a writer knows how to achieve a certain effect, the method must be abandoned. Effects repeated become false, mannered. The writer's style is his doppelgänger, an apparition that the writer must never trust to do his work for him.

Some years ago I began writing essays. They were strident, bitter pieces on topics I cared about deeply. I developed a certain style for them that was unlike the style of my stories — it was unelusive and rude and brashly one-sided. They were meant to annoy and trouble and polarize, and they made readers, at least the kind of readers who write letters to the editors of magazines, half nuts with rage and disdain. The letter-writers frequently mocked my name. Not only didn't they like my way with words, my reasoning, my philosophy, they didn't believe my name. My morbid attitude, my bitter tongue, my anger, denied me the right to such a name, my given name, my gift, signifier of rejoicing, happiness, and delight.

But a writer isn't supposed to make friends with his writing, I don't think.

The writer doesn't trust his enemies, of course, who are wrong about his writing, but he doesn't trust his friends, either, who he hopes are right. The writer trusts nothing he writes — it should be too reckless and alive for that, it should be beautiful and menacing and slightly out of his control. It should want to live itself somehow. The writer dies — he can die before he dies, it happens all the time, he dies as a writer — but the work wants to live.

Language accepts the writer as its host, it feeds off the writer, it makes him a husk. There is something uncanny about good writing — uncanny the singing that comes from certain husks. The writer is never nourished by his own work, it is never satisfying to him. The work is a stranger, it shuns him a little, for the writer is really something of a fool, so engaged in his disengagement, so self-conscious, so eager to serve something greater, which is the writing. Or which could be the writing if only the writer is good enough. The work stands a little apart from the writer, it doesn't want to go down with him when he stumbles or fails or retreats.

The writer must do all this alone, in secret, in drudgery, in confusion, awkwardly, one word at a time.

The writer is an exhibitionist, and yet he is private. He wants you to admire his fasting, his art. He wants your attention, he doesn't want you to know he exists. The reality of his life is meaningless, why should you, the reader, care? You don't care. He drinks, he loves unwisely, he's happy, he's sick . . . it doesn't matter. You just want the work — the Other — this other thing. You don't really care how he does it. Why he does it.

The good piece of writing startles the reader back into Life. The work — this Other, this other thing — this false life that is even less than the seeming of this lived life, is more than the lived life, too. It is so unreal, so precise, so unsurprising, so alarming, really. Good writing never soothes or comforts. It is no prescription, neither is it diversionary, although it can and should enchant while it explodes in the reader's face. Whenever the writer writes, it's always three o'clock in the morning, it's always three or four or five o'clock in the morning in his head. Those horrid hours are the writer's days and nights when he is writing. The writer doesn't write for the reader. He doesn't write for himself, either. He writes to serve . . . something. Somethingness. The somethingness that is sheltered by the wings of nothingness — those exquisite, enveloping, protecting wings.

There is a little tale about man's fate and this is the way it is put. A man is being pursued by a raging elephant and takes refuge in a tree at the edge of a fearsome abyss. Two mice, one black and one white, are gnawing at the roots of the tree, and at the bottom of the abyss is a dragon with parted jaws. The man looks above and sees a little honey trickling down the tree and he begins to lick it up and forgets his perilous situation. But the mice gnaw through the tree and the man falls down and the elephant seizes him and hurls him over to the dragon. Now, that elephant is the image of death, which pursues men, and the tree is this transitory existence, and the mice are the days and the nights, and the honey is the sweetness of the passing world, and the savor of the passing world diverts mankind. So the days and nights are accomplished and death seizes him and the dragon swallows him down into hell and this is the life of man.

This little tale with its broad and beastly strokes seems to approximate man's dilemma quite charmingly, with the added caveat that it also applies to the ladies ("she" being "he" throughout here, the writer's woes not limited by gender; like Flannery O'Connor's Misfit, the writer knows there's no enjoyment to be had in this life). This is the story, then, pretty much the story, with considerable latitude to be had in describing those mice, those terrifying mice. But it is not for the writer to have any part in providing the honey — the passing world does that. The writer can't do better than that. What the writer wants to do, to be, is to be the consciousness of the story, he doesn't want to be part of the distraction; to distract is ignoble, to distract is to admit defeat, to serve a lesser god. The story is not a simple one. It is syncretistic and strange and unhappy, and it all must be told beautifully, even the horrible parts, particularly the horrible parts. The telling of the story can never end, not because the writer doesn't like the way it must end but because there is no end to the awareness of the story which the writer has only the dimmest, most fragmentary awareness of.

Why do I write? Writing has never given me any pleasure. I am not being disingenuous here. It's not a matter of being on excellent terms with my characters, having a swell time with them, finding their surprising remarks prescient or amusing. That would seem to be a shallow pleasure indeed. Rewriting, the attention to detail, the depth of involvement required, the achievement and acknowledgment of the prowess and stamina and luck involved — all these should give their pleasures, I suppose, but they are sophisticated pleasures that elude me. Writing has never been "fun" for me. I am too wary about writing to enjoy it. It has never fulfilled me (nor have I fulfilled it). Writing has never done anyone or anything any good at all, as far as I can tell. In the months before my mother died, and she was so sick and at home, a home that meant everything and nothing to her now, she said that she would lie awake through the nights and plan the things she would do during the day when it came — she would walk the dog and get birdseed and buy some more pansies, and she would make herself a nice little breakfast, something that would taste good, a poached egg and some toast — and then the day would come and she could do none of these things, she could not even get out the broom and sweep a little. She was in such depression and such pain and she would cry, If I only could do a little sweeping, just that. . . . To sweep with a good broom, a lovely thing, such a simple, satisfying thing, and she yearned to do it and could not. And her daughter, the writer, who would be the good broom quick in her hands if only she were able, could not help her in any way. Nothing the daughter, the writer, had ever written or could ever write could help my mother who had named me.

Why does the writer write? The writer writes to serve — hopelessly he writes in the hope that he might serve — not himself and not others, but that great cold elemental grace which knows us.

A writer I very much admire is Don DeLillo. At an awards ceremony for him at the Folger Library several years ago, I said that he was like a great shark moving hidden in our midst, beneath the din and wreck of the moment, at apocalyptic ease in the very elements of our psyche and times that are most troublesome to us, that we most fear.

Why do I write? Because I wanna be a great shark too. Another shark. A different shark, in a different part of the ocean. The ocean is vast.

Where Does
Writing Come From?

RICHARD FORD

⤙⤚

Our brains are dulled by the incurable mania of
wanting to make the unknown known.
ANDRÉ BRETON, *The Surrealist Manifesto*

I'VE OFTEN BEEN GUILTY of trying to answer the question
above. I've done it on public stages after readings, in panel dis-
cussions with dozing colleagues, standing before rows of smirking
students, for cruel and cynical journalists in hotel rooms at home
and abroad. And I believe I can honestly say that I would never
spontaneously have asked myself this question had not someone
else seemed interested, or had my financial fortunes not seemed
(correctly or incorrectly) tied to such speculation. I either knew
the answer, I suppose, or thought I didn't need to know it. Yet
once the question was asked, I admit that over these years I've

taken an interest in the answers I've come up with — which is to say, dreamed up — much in the way I take interest in the progress of any piece of fiction I'm writing. This, after all, is what one does, or what I do, anyway, when I write fiction: pick out something far-fetched or at least previously unthought of by me, something I feel a kind of languageless yen for, and then see what I can dream up about it or around it that's interesting or amusing to me, in the hope that by making it make sense in words I'll make it interesting and important to someone else.

Plenty of writers for plenty of centuries have furrowed their brows over this question — where does it come from, all this stuff you write? "All good poetry is the spontaneous overflow of powerful feelings" was an important part of Wordsworth's answer. And I've seen no reason I shouldn't just as well get my two cents down, on the chance I might actually get to or near the bottom of the whole subject and possibly help extinguish literature once and for all — since that seems to be where the inquiry tends: let's get writing explained and turned into a neat theorem, like a teasing problem in plasma physics, so we can forget about it and get back to watching *Seinfeld*. And failing that, I might at least say something witty or charming that could make a listener or a reader seek out the book I really do care about — the one I've just written and hope you'll love.

It may be that this investigation stays alive in America partly because of that principally American institution, the creative-writing course — of which I am a bona fide graduate, and about which Europeans like to roll their eyes. The institution has many virtues — time to write being the most precious. But it also has several faults, one of which is the unproven good of constantly having like-minded colleagues and compatriots around to talk about what one is doing, as if companionship naturally improved one's important work just when one is doing it. How we do what we do, and why we do it, may just be a subject a certain kind of anxious person can't help tumbling to at a time in life when getting things written at all is a worry, and when one's body of work is small and not very distinguishable from one's private self, and when one comes to find that the actual thing one is writing is not a very riveting topic of conversation over drinks. Among dedicated novices, the large subject of provenance may be all we have in common, and all that will pass for artily abstract speculation of a disinterested kind.

Though clearly another socioliterary force that keeps the topic alive is that among many people who are *not* writers, there's occasionally a flighty belief that writers are special people, vergers of some kind, in charge of an important interior any person would be wise to come close to as a way of sidling up to a potent life's essence. Questions about how, why, etc., become just genuflections before the medium. And writers, being generally undercharged in self-esteem and forever wanting more attention for their work, are often quite willing to become their work's exponent if not its actual avatar. I remember an anecdote about a male writer I know who, upon conducting an interested visitor to his desk overlooking the Pacific, is reported to have whispered as they tiptoed into the sacred, sun-shot room, "Well, here it is. This is where I make the magic."

Again, nothing's new here: just another instance of supposing an approach upon the writer will reveal the written thing more fully, more truly; or, if not, then it's the old mistake of confusing the maker with the made thing — an object that may really have some magical pizzazz about it, who knows?

Considering an actual set of mechanical connections that might have brought a piece of writing from nowhere, the "place" it resided before I'd written it, to its final condition as the book I hope you'll love, actually impresses upon me the romantic view that artistic invention is a kind of casual magic, one that can't be adequately explained the way, say, a train's arrival in Des Moines can be nicely accounted for by tracing the tracks and switches and sidings and tunnels all the way to its origin in Paducah.

You can — and scholars do — try to trace some apparent connections back from the finished work to the original blank mind and page and even to before that (he used his father's name for the ax-murderer . . . hmmm; she suffered glaucoma just like the jilted sister who became a Carmelite nun, so how can you argue the whole damn story isn't about moral blindness?). But of course such procedures are famously unreliable and even sometimes downright impertinent, since in the first place (and there need not be a second) such investigations start at and take for granted the existence of Des Moines, whereas for the writer (and I mean to abandon this train business), Des Moines is not just a city but a name that has to be not merely found, but conjured. In fact the name may not even have been Des Moines to begin with — it may have been Abilene or Chagrin Falls — but *became* Des Moines because the writer somehow slipped up and let Abilene slip his mind, or because Des Moines had that nice diphthong in it and looked neat and Frenchy on the page, whereas Abilene had those three clunky syllables, and there was already a dopey country song about it. Anyway, there are at least two Abilenes, one in Texas and another one in Kansas, which is confusing, and neither has rail service.

You can see what I mean: the true connections could never really be traceable because they exist only in that murky, silent, but fecund interstellar night where impulse, free association, instinct, and error reign. And even if I were faithfully to try explaining the etiological connections in a piece of writing I'd done, I still might lie about them, or I might just be wrong because I forgot. But in any case I'd finally have to make something up pretty much the way a scholar does — though not exactly like a writer, who, as I said before, always starts with nothing.

I remember a complimentary reviewer of a book I'd written once singling out for approval my choice of adjectives, which seemed to him surprising and expansive and of benefit to the story. One sentence he liked contained a phrase in which I'd referred to a character's eyes as "old": "He looked on her in an old-eyed way." Naturally, I was pleased to have written *something* that *somebody* liked. Only, when I was not long afterward packing away manuscripts for the attic, my eyes happened to fall upon the page and the very commended phrase, "old-eyed," etc., and I noticed that somehow in the rounds of fatigued retyping that used to precede a writer's final sign-off on a book in the days before word processors, the original and rather dully hybridized "cold-eyed" had somehow lost its c and become "old-eyed," only nobody'd noticed since they both made a kind of sense.

This is my larger point writ, admittedly, small, and it calls to mind the joke about the man from Alabama who couldn't understand how a thermos could keep cold things cold and hot things always hot, and expressed his wonder in a question akin to the title of this very essay: "How do it know?"

Anyone who's ever written a novel or a story or a poem and had the occasion later to converse about it with an agitated or merely interested reader knows the pinchy feel that comes when the reader tries to nail down the connections *linking* the story to some supposed "source," as a way either of illuminating the procedures that transform life to shapely art, or else of just plain diminishing an act of creation to some problem of industrial design.

In my case, this inquiry often centers on the potent subject of children, and specifically writing about children, and more prosecutorily on how it is *I* can write about children to such and such effect without actually having or having had any myself.

It's frequently surprising to whomever I'm speaking to that I can write persuasively about children; although the surprise is often expressed not as pure delight but in a kind of blinkingly suspicious tone whose spirit is either that I *do* have children (in another county, maybe) and don't want to admit it, or else that somebody in a position of authority needs to come down and take a closer look at my little minor inventions to certify if they're really as finely drawn as they seem.

Myself, I try to stay happy about such questioning. Some stranger, after all, *has* or *seems to have* read at least a part of some book I've written and been moved by it, and I'm always grateful for that. He or she could as easily have been watching *Seinfeld*, too. And so mostly I just try to smile and chuckle and mumble-mutter something about having been a child once myself, and if that doesn't work I say something about there being children pretty much everywhere for the watchful to study, and that my Jamesian job is to be a good observer. And finally, if that still isn't enough, I say that if it were so hard to write about children, I of all people wouldn't be able to do it, since I'm no smarter than the next guy.

But the actual truth — the one I know to be true and that sustains my stories — is that even though I was once a child myself, and even though there is a God's own slew of bratty kids around to be studied like lab rats, and even though I'm clearly not the smartest man in the world, I still mostly write about children by making them up. I make them up out of language bits, out of my memories, out of stories in the newspapers, out of overheard remarks by my friends and their kids, out of this and out of that, and sometimes out of nothing at all but the pleasurable will to ascribe something that might be interesting on the page to a child instead of to an adult or a spaceman or a horse, after which a *child*, a fictive child, begins to take shape on the page as a willed, moral gesture toward the reader. "'All I want for Christmas is to know the difference between *that* and *which*,' said little Johnny, who was just ten years old but already beginning to need some firmer discipline." Behold: a child is born.

Occasionally, if pushed or annoyed, I'll come right out and say it: *I make these little buggers up, that's what. So sue me.* But an odd restraint almost always makes me revert to my prior explanations. Some delicacy in me simply doesn't want to say, "They're invented things, these characters; you can't track them down like rabbits to their holes. They won't be hiding there." It's as though arguing for invention and its fragile, wondrous efficacy were indelicate, weren't quite nice. And even though arguing for it wouldn't harm or taint invention's marvels (we all know novels are made-up things; it's part of our pleasure to keep such knowledge in our minds), still I always feel queasy doing it — not like a magician who reluctantly shows a rube how to pull a nickel out of his own ear, but more like a local parish priest who, upon hearing a small but humiliating confession from a friend, lets the friend off easy just to move matters on to a higher ground.

Wallace Stevens once wrote that "in an age of disbelief . . . it is for the poet to supply the satisfactions of belief in his measure and his style." And that takes in how I feel about invention — invented characters, invented landscapes, invented breaks of the heart and their subsequent repairs. I believe that there are important made-up things that resist precise tracing back, and that it's a blessing there are, since our acceptance of them in literature (acting as a substitute for less acceptable beliefs) suggests that for every human problem, every insoluble, every cul-de-sac, every despair, there's a chance we can conjure up an improvement — a Des Moines where previously there was only a glum Abilene.

Frank Kermode wrote thirty years ago, in his wonderful book *The Sense of an Ending*, "It is not that we are connoisseurs of chaos, but that we are surrounded by it, and equipped for coexistence with it only by our fictive powers." To my mind, not to believe in invention, in our fictive powers, but instead to think that all is traceable, that the rabbit must finally be in the hole waiting, is (because it's dead wrong) a certain recipe for the williwaws of disappointment and a small but needless reproach to mankind's saving capacity to imagine what could be better and, with good hope, then, to seek it.

I Am a . . . *Genius!*

THOM JONES

As a fiction instructor at the University of Iowa, I was often asked by my students what it takes to devise a "breakthrough" short story or novel. Something to skyrocket the writer to fame and fortune, set the literary world aglow, win a ton of prizes, and guarantee the author a rich and prosperous future. I was a student at the Workshop myself back in the seventies, and it was a question I had dwelled on like a Zen koan. I used to think about it so hard my brain started smoking. I was Smokin' Thom Jones. Did I smoke cigarettes? No, but I was Smokin' Thom Jones. I smoked, smoldered, and fumed so hard I had to duct-tape ice cubes alongside my temporal lobes to prevent my whole head from bursting into flames, luxurious, gorgeous, flowing chestnut locks and all. It was the most acutely awful taxing of my brain that I had ever put it to in a voluntary fashion. And what did I come up with? I came up with zip. No miracles, just commonplace notions. I figured that not only did you actually have to write to become a writer, but there was probably also a trick to the whole affair. Possibly there was a secret mystical society you had to join. At the least, I imagined that it had something to do with giving the right people "blow jobs." Beyond that, I was clueless. While other Iowa writers were hanging out at the Mill or the Foxhead, my fingers were blistering the keyboard five hours a day, seven days a week. I was just another greaseball from Aurora, Illinois, but I had my dreams. I believed. And I churned out one boring novel after another. The all-consuming urge to write novels began years before, when I was just a kid reading comic books in the back of my grandmother's grocery store.

Like most of the people reading this piece, I was subjected to the gulag of the American school system — not the light-duty mainstream but the maximum-security variant of such. It was a Missouri synod Lutheran school, where educational training was presented not as an opportunity but rather as a sentence to be served — a grim fourteen-year term that made Turkish prison seem like a lark and Kaspar Hauser's early incarceration an idyllic haven of uninterrupted bliss.

I tuned out in passive/aggressive style and earned very low marks. From browsing at pictures in my geography texts, I knew there were "born-free" kids in exotic parts of the world who were accorded instant adulthood. Instead of going to school, they might herd goats near the Kyber Pass, slog through sun-torched mosquito days in Burmese rice paddies, mash cassava down in the tropics, or, way up in latitude 87, where it was cold enough to freeze the balls off a brass monkey, make mukluks out of sealskin. They looked like very happy kids. They were smiling, and there wasn't an ambiguous shit-eating grin in the bunch, no smile that implicitly said, "I had to dish out seven hundred blow jobs to land this gig — suck every cock on the North Pole — but *here I am*, brother. Now ain't this . . . *real fine?*" Judging by that grin on your face, Nanook, I would say it's mighty fine indeed.

There I was at the age of reason, a *seldom* smiler — an *on-rare-occasions-only* smiler —knowing that it was theoretically possible to steal away from my bedroom one night and reemerge as a fair-eyed nomad on camel caravan in the Sahara or as an aboriginal on walkabout through the deserts of western Australia, far from the influence of crass materialism and the soul-withering zone of capitalistic imperialism that were part and parcel of the Eisenhower fifties.

The Lutheran elementary school was run by stern, joyless, second-generation German authoritarians, a Paraguay in the Midwest where crowd control was maintained by repressive conditioning and the iron fist of fear. My defense against this bullshit turn of fate was rebellion. I was a regular little James Cagney in those days.

I was an evildoer of the first order, a recidivist troublemaker who spent many long lunch hours in the principal's office (P-Block), surreptitiously drawing comics while the other students were allowed to exercise out on the "yard." My skills as an artist were rudimentary, but my ability to capture the essential horrors of Aurora, Illinois, was Hogarthian. Yes, dear reader, I was a genius even then!

On paper my wit was rapier-sharp, and the students who were privileged to view my work were known to fall down laughing or even piss in their pants. Yet when these "subversive" documents found their way into the hands of the authorities, I drew even more time in P-Block. The school's headmaster gave my mother the name of a "head doctor," and I was sent to see him. He thought my comics were piss-in-your-pants funny, too, and would sit in his office pounding his fist against his thigh as he read them, roaring with laughter. He would have to blow his nose and dab his eyes after these convulsions of mirth. Then he would remember he was a psychiatrist and would say, "Your problem, my young friend, is this: you are a stubborn individualist. You want to go it alone in the ant colony of society, and that just isn't possible. Most likely you will end up dead at an early age, or in prison. Already you are addicted to comic books; you even make your own. While they are funny, the themes emerging from them are the product of a disturbed mind. Why don't you join the Boy Scouts and get a little fresh air or something?"

I said there were two things I hated to do: get up before four P.M. and go outside.

He shook his head and said, "If that's the case, you might as well shoot yourself and get it over with now. You're in for a lot of pain and heartache, my little buddy, for you are going to find this planet a cruel and brutal place."

Each month when my grandmother received a new shipment of comics at her store, by the strictest self-imposed rationing schedule, I found myself with three days of pure reading pleasure. I wasn't one of those geniuses who were reading Vladimir Nabokov when they were six. I was reading Little Lulu. What I had seen passed off as literature was tedious and dull. Few of the literary offerings presented to us in school made for pleasant reading. They were sheer drudgery. James Fenimore Cooper comes to mind. And the poem *Hiawatha*.

That all changed when I happened upon a copy of *Huckleberry Finn*. I liked Mark Twain and attacked his whole body of work. Then one thing led to another. As an omnivorous reader of comic books, I easily accomplished the transition to reading books of all kinds. My favorites were works of fiction inhabited by characters

of alienation. I prowled the glass-floored balcony of the Aurora public library, reading such authors as Steinbeck, Dickens, Somerset Maugham, Jack London, and Kenneth Roberts for no reason other than information and pleasure. My criminal mind was not bent on self-improvement, but reading did have a side benefit: it did not lead to pregnancies, hangovers, beatings, or arrests. By high school I was reading John Updike and Kingsley Amis — hardly a precocious feat, unless you think of Aurora in terms of that awful gold pit they've got in the Brazilian jungle, and imagine the shantytown culture that flourishes around it. All Aurora had going for it was a Carnegie-vintage library. It was otherwise a town devoid of color.

At the library I made the acquaintance of Salinger, who influenced me greatly, and, if I remember correctly, it was Salinger who suggested that being an author of fiction was the most noble occupation of all. Hemingway, who came from not-so-distant Oak Park, Illinois, was America's larger-than-life writer at this time. But though he wrote of things that fascinated me, like war, bullfighting, and boxing, I was never a diehard Hemingway fan. I did not dispute his authority; I just liked other writers better — Nelson Algren and James Jones, for instance. Jones was the one author I ever sent a fan letter to (I received a gracious response). I loved William Styron, John Dos Passos, and Norman Mailer. I loved Joyce Carol Oates, who did not strut and swagger but instead put out a prodigious amount of really good work. I was not a snob. I expected that I would spend my life working in one of the many factories in Aurora, Illinois. But my God, what hellholes those factories were! As my high school graduation approached, I let my subscription to Ace Comics slide past its renewal date. I didn't require pictures any longer; I was addicted to words.

*   *   *

Since none of my friends were readers, I found my own way. *Lucky Jim* had a great impact on me. There was Alan Sillitoe with *Loneliness of the Long-Distance Runner* and *Saturday Night and Sunday Morning; Alfie* by Bill Naughton; *The Luck of Ginger Coffee* by Brian Moore; *Poor Cow* by Nell Dunn; *Room at the Top* and the whole body of work by John Braine. I read Flannery O'Connor, Carson McCullers, Theodore Dreiser. A fellow I knew at a warehouse job handed me a copy of *Vandover and the Brute*, a lesser novel by Frank Norris. *Vandover* instantly soared to my topten list. This was almost immediately surpassed by Par Lagerkvist's *The Dwarf*. My new reading buddy belt-fed real beauties to me: Stendhal's *The Red and the Black*; Jules Reynard's *Pol de Carrot*; V. S. Naipaul's *A House for Mr. Biswas*; Flaubert's *Madame Bovary*; and *Revolutionary Road* by Richard Yates.

I finally escaped the factories of Aurora and went to the University of Hawaii. Through a stroke of luck, I got a small apartment in an exclusive Manoa Valley subdivision by working as my landlady's gardener. There were royal palms off my lanai, and gardenia trees that blew fragrant breezes into my apartment each night. I signed up for my first course in creative writing, and with the trade winds blowing off the heat of each day, I pounded a Royal standard typewriter late into the night. Just as I had once found remission from the existential chasm of despair in the act of writing comics, I now found the same relief in writing fiction. *Esquire* and the *Atlantic Monthly* asked for rewrites on the first two stories I wrote. These were fixes I didn't even attempt since I felt I was light-years beyond them. I was already hard at work on a novel.

Ultimately I entered the writing program at Iowa, where a friend put me onto Hubert Selby's *Last Exit to Brooklyn*, a book that was to influence me profoundly. After Iowa I took my first trip to Europe and began to hunger after travel. I worked at an assortment of writing jobs and found them meaningless and debilitating. Any thoughts I had of becoming a real writer were extinguished soon after I joined the American work force. When I returned to Iowa to teach, I saw my students face their own graduations with a dread of the real world that bordered on panic. It was perceived as something that could suck you into its vortex and never let you go. It was a Venus's-flytrap that ate out your soul.

But life gives you many chances. After getting fired from a job as a newspaper editor in 1980, I wrote another unpublishable novel. I didn't even send it out. I got drunk and burned it.

I was drinking heavily at the time and counteracting this destructive pastime with twenty-mile runs, three-mile swims, three-hour weight-lifting sessions. I was still boxing, in spite of my epilepsy. There was a good angel perched on one shoulder and a bad one on the other.

When I ran out of money, I took a job as a night janitor at a school, where I had a pool, a weight room, a library all to myself. It was a great thing. I could rush through my area in a few hours and after that I was free to pursue whatever pleasures that struck my fancy. I was still addicted to compulsive exercise and it was for this reason that I had taken the job. One night, with a case of beer at hand, I did ten thousand sit-ups in sets of five hundred. It was easy, although I think it wrecked my back forever. In those days I could do thirty-five chin-ups, press 138 pounds behind the neck, and curl 125 pounds in reps of eight. I could pick up the entire stack of weights on the Universal machine. Weight lifting merely requires a doggedness bordering on obsession. After two years of this, nearly every joint in my body was injured. Drinking killed the pain and tedium of it, but long-term sprains would force me into weeks of recuperation. I kept on drinking. My hand-to-mouth action was never impaired, and the drinking got out of hand. There were close calls. I had to open up the school and was often drunk by then. My partner on the graveyard shift was a pot smoker, and by dawn we looked like a pair of Mission Street bums. Our eyes were like two balls of fire. There were Visine bottles everywhere you turned, and the hangovers were like bad mescaline trips. Ultimately the drinking pushed me into type 1 diabetes, and I had no choice but to stop. Stop on a dime, bro! From the first, sobriety did not seem like a very friendly place. I could accomplish only a small amount of physical work and would then be forced to lie on the floor for a time to recover from these small exertions. I would maybe get up, look in the mirror to see one pupil fully dilated and the other a pinpoint. I think they call it Horner's symptom, evidence of an ongoing stroke. My heart would flutter like a Hong Kong chicken suffering bird flu. I would go down to the welding shop and inhale pure oxygen until my sickly, racing pulse sank back into the double-digit area. The man of ten thousand sit-ups now barely had the strength to get through a single night of work. I switched over to the second shift to ensure that I would not fall off the wagon — there were too many people around then for me to get away with drinking. Also, if I fell down dead on the second shift, I was reasonably certain that my body would be found and my family notified.

Friday was the worst of days since every week feeds a janitor a furious succession of psychic blows. The students become more and more restless, and by Fridays, they are wild. Also, Friday was the night I would empty the bag on my commercial vacuum cleaner. In less than a week it would accumulate ten or fifteen pounds of dust. It was necessary to shake it into the Dumpster, but hair and fibers fallen onto the carpets caused the bag dust to adhere together into Velcro-like clumps. To avoid breathing in the dust particles, I would hold my breath and reach elbow-deep into the bag to pull out the dirt. It was like working in a flour factory. By the time I had the bulky stuff pulled out, I would be covered with filth, and as often as not, my fingers would be sliced from the pins, paper clips, and used hypodermic syringes that waited for my hands like Cracker Jack prizes in the compacted dust. It was exasperating. Just a complete motherfucker.

And I still wasn't finished. Under the cover of darkness, I repaired to a fence by the agriculture shop, where I would beat the bag against a fence post. This would clear the bag of the finer dust particles. I looked like a maniac chopping logs. I hacked and slammed the bag, and with every faceful of dust, the madder I got. Each bag-blow against the fence released huge gusts of filth into the atmosphere. Once, on a football night, I unleashed a facsimile of the Bikini Island atomic mushroom cloud, watched it rise five hundred feet into the air, and then soar over the football field, where the game was in progress. I heard the crowd gasp collectively in awe. It was a rainy night, and up near the klieg lights, some thousand yards away, the sinister dust ball hovered like the wrath of God — like impending doom.

Since I knew this would draw an immediate investigation, I hastened back into the building and casually resumed my routine. When a pair of cops came inside and asked me if I had been "out back" recently or seen anything strange, I said no. I lied again when the vice principal came inside and said people were complaining because every car in the parking lot was covered with a thick brown-and-gray paste having the consistency of cold gravy. I gave him a quizzical look and said, "Well, maybe Mount Saint Helens blew again."

"No," he said. "I remember *that*, and this is worse. Far worse!"

I looked at him like, "Hey, man, don't get all bent out of shape. You should have *my* fucking job."

I didn't know how many more Friday nights I had left in me. Once I offered another janitor a hundred dollars if he would dump my bag, and he refused. I considered other employment options, but it occurred to me that I wasn't very good at anything. I had hated every job I'd ever had.

Then one day, watching television, I saw Wile E. Coyote chasing the Road Runner across a cartoon desert. Cartoon New Mexico, I figure. I was hoping that he would catch the stupid and annoying bird and rip its head off. But then, in the middle of the chase, the coyote came to a screeching halt, stepped out of the cartoon, and walked toward the audience with a wry, self-satisfied grin on his face. His footfalls ka-flop ka-flop ka-flop, cartoon style. No big hurry here. He acted like he had all the time in the world. When he was finally in place, he pulled his shoulders back, looked into the camera, and said, just as cool as you please, "Allow me to introduce myself. Wile E. Coyote . . . *genius.*"

"Genius," he said. Genniiee-us. *Genieuz.* Maybe that's just another word for perseverance. Wile E. Coyote, no matter what else you might say about him, was not a quitter. I mean, if you keep plugging at it, you *might* get it. If you quit — pow, it's over.

Maybe it was my comic-book past — those lost years of happiness — that caused me to be affected so deeply. Wile E. Coyote reinvigorated me with hope. I made up my mind to take another stab at writing. At the time I was reading and rereading some very good writers, including Raymond Carver, Tobias Wolff, Robert Stone, Michael Herr, Richard Price, Larry Brown, and Cormac McCarthy — immaculate writers, immortals. I decided to forget trying to imitate any of them. Part of a writer's style is always imbued with the styles of the people he reads, but to the extent that such a thing was possible, I determined to write for myself alone. I would write the sort of material that pleased me, and this meant dwelling on life's absurdities. I bought a Macintosh computer. Because of my work schedule and diminished health, I wrote stories. You can write a short story in a sitting, say on a Saturday afternoon. With a draft done and the mood, atmosphere, and tone of the piece captured in the first stroke, I didn't have to try and pick up the voice again and sustain it through further adventures — all I had to do was rewrite and polish. It was fun from the very beginning. Va-room! Va-room! No more lying on the floor before the TV Saturday afternoons waiting for hangovers to burn off for Thom; I was writing. Self-discipline became my middle name. Before the Mac, I had never written more than three drafts of anything. Now I was a rewriting ace. My first computer-written piece was "Rocketman," a story about professional boxing. I went through something like thirty drafts and then I sent it to Jon Jackson, an Iowa pal and a writer who had earned a living from writing almost from the day he left the Workshop. Jon knows a lot about boxing, and he liked the story. He showed it to Richard Ford, who thought Joyce Oates might like it for the *Ontario Review*. No oral sex was asked for or given. I got a nice note from Ms. Oates, one of my great heroes. It was the first personal note I'd received since *Esquire* and the *Atlantic* wrote me in Hawaii back in the sixties. I made some changes and returned the story to the *Ontario Review*. Ultimately, it was turned down, and I was overcome by a tsunami wave of self-pity. The Voice of Discouragement spoke to me from one of my Friday-night dust clouds: "You ain't got it, man. You might as well go and buy a case of beer. You're just a greaseball. A janitor. Aurora, Illinois. Shame on you!"

I told Jon Jackson I couldn't write any better than that. He said,

"Thom, look, you wrote one of the best goddamn boxing stories I ever read. But remember this: editors don't want to *buy* your stories. They get tons of stories. *You have to write something that's so good they can't reject it.* This isn't about connections or whom you know. It's about the text. Nine times out of ten, a good magazine will print a first-rate story by an unknown before they run a second-rate story by a marquee name."

"They will?" I said.

I still remember Jackson's exasperation. "Thom!" he said. "For Christ's sake!"

His words were golden. I felt like Grasshopper in *Kung Fu*, getting some big-time insight. Suddenly acceptance wasn't about me; it was about the text. I wasn't so sure I could overcome my low self-esteem, but I truly believed I could write something fresh, original, unlike anything anyone else had ever written — something *sui generis*. Jackson had effectively severed the connection between my talent and my personal self-perceptions. I said, "Why didn't you tell me this shit twenty-five years ago?"

I felt like a *genieuz* again. A genius with a difference. Writing straight from the heart, I sat down and composed "The Pugilist at Rest" in a single sitting. Three days later I wrote "I Want to Live," and so it went. One afternoon my then-agent, Candida Donadio, called me up three times in rapid succession: first to report a sale to *Harper's*; thirty minutes later another sale, to *Esquire*; and then, fifteen minutes after that, yet another, to the *New Yorker*. Three in an afternoon. She said, "Thirty years in the business, and I've never seen that happen. Never."

As it turned out, all three of the magazines hit the newsstands in the same month, and passing through an airport I saw them on a magazine rack — all three in my frame of vision. I had been in the slicks frequently since the publication of "Pugilist," but I did not live in New York and was virtually unknown there. People were saying, "Who the fuck is this guy?" To the reading public it seemed like overnight success, but fiction writers often mature at a glacial pace. I was slower than most. I was sometimes on the verge of agreeing with Stanislavsky, who said, "They are most happy who have no story to tell." After getting lost and being found time and again, the writers who don't quit discover the ecstasy within the process of the work itself. They discover the sublime joy of seeing things come together to produce an artistic whole. You read books and love them and someday hope to have the talent and vision to write your own. It doesn't matter who you are or where you come from. In fact, many of our best writers come from the streets. From places like Aurora, Illinois. You can be a greaseball off the streets, so long as you are a greaseball who knows how to put things together. Fame or money might follow, but they are never the primary event. I had a lot of students tell me they were going to cop out and write screenplays or genre fiction to "make a shitload of money." And my reply was always the same: You don't just toss things off and make money. You have to write with your heart and soul. Do you think Willie Mays played center field for the Giants just so he could become rich and famous? Or do you think maybe he played it because he loved the game? Loved it so much he would have done it for free?

Someday Wile E. Coyote will prevail. Not because he wants a bird sandwich, but because he has a burning desire. He will pay the price. He will go the extra mile. And one day he will find the right plan. I know he will. That wolf is a *genieuz*.

Some for Glory, Some for Praise

JAMES SALTER

"To write! What a marvelous thing!" When he was old and forgotten, living in a rundown house in the dreary suburbs of Paris, Léautaud wrote these lines. He was unmarried, childless, alone. The world of the theater in which he had worked as a critic for years was now dark for him, but from the ruins of his life these words rose. *To write!*

One thinks of many writers who might have said this, Anne Sexton, even though she committed suicide, or Hemingway or Virginia Woolf, who both did also, or Faulkner, scorned in his rural town, or the wreckage that was Fitzgerald in the end. The thing that is marvelous is literature, which is like the sea, and the exaltation of being near it, whether you are a powerful swimmer or wading by the shore. The act of writing, though often tedious, can still provide extraordinary pleasure. For me that comes line by line at the tip of a pen, which is what I like to write with, and the page on which the lines are written, the pages, can be the most valuable thing I will ever own.

The cynics say that if you do not write for money you are a dabbler or a fool, but this is not true. To see one's work in print is the real desire, to have it read. The remuneration is of less importance; no one was paid for the samizdats. Money is but one form of approval.

It is such a long time that I have been writing that I don't remember the beginning. It was not a matter of doing what my father knew how to do. He had gone to Rutgers, West Point, and then MIT, and I don't think in my lifetime I ever saw him reading a novel. He read newspapers, the *Sun*, the *World-Telegram*, there were at least a dozen in New York in those days. His task was laid out for him: to rise in the world.

Nor was my mother an avid reader. She read to me as a child, of course, and in time I read the books that were published in popular series, *The Hardy Boys* and *Bomba, the Jungle Boy*. I recall little about them. I did not read *Ivanhoe*, *Treasure Island*, *Kim*, or *The Scottish Chiefs*, though two or three of them were given to me. I had six volumes of a collection called *My Bookhouse*, edited by Olive Beaupré Miller, whose name is not to be found among the various Millers — Mrs. Alice, Henry, Joaquin, Joe — in *The Reader's Encyclopedia*, but who was responsible for what knowledge I had of Cervantes, Dickens, Tolstoy, Homer, and the others whose work was excerpted. The contents also included folktales, fairy tales, parts of the Bible, and more. When I read of writers who when young were given the freedom of their fathers' or friends' libraries, I think of *Bookhouse*, which was that for me. It was not an education but the introduction to one.

There were also poems, and in grammar school we had to memorize and then stand up and recite well-known poems. Many of these I still know, including Kipling's "If," which my father paid me a dollar to learn. Language is acquired, like other things, through the act of imitating, and rhythm and elegance may come in part from poems.

I could draw quite well as a boy and even, though uninstructed, paint. What impulse made me do this, and where the ability came from — although my father could draw a little — I cannot say. My desire to write, apparent at the age of seven or eight, likely came from the same source. I made crude books, as many children do, with awkward printing and drawings, from small sheets of paper, folded and sewn together.

In prep school we were poets, at least many of my friends and I were, ardent and profound. There were elegies but no love poems — those came later. I had some early success. In a national poetry contest I won honorable mention, and sold two poems to *Poetry* magazine.

All this was a phase, in nearly every case to be soon outgrown. In 1939 the war had broken out, and by 1941 we were in it. I ended up at West Point. The old life vanished; the new one had little use for poetry. I did read, and as an upperclassman wrote a few short stories. I had seen some in the Academy magazine and felt I could do better, and after the first one, the editor asked for more. When I became an officer there was, at first, no time for writing, nor was there the privacy. Beyond that was a greater inhibition: it was alien to the life. I had been commissioned in the Army Air Force and in the early days was a transport pilot, later switching into fighters. With that I felt I had found my role.

Stationed in Florida in about 1950, I happened to see in a bookshop window in Pensacola a boldly displayed novel called *The Town and the City* by John Kerouac. The name. There had been a Jack Kerouac at prep school, and he had written some stories.

On the back of the jacket was a photograph, a gentle, almost yearning face with eyes cast downward. I recognized it instantly. I remember a feeling of envy. Kerouac was only a few years older than I was. Somehow he had written this impressive-looking novel. I bought the book and eagerly read it. It owed a lot to Thomas Wolfe — *Look Homeward, Angel* and others — who was a major figure then, but still it was an achievement. I took it as a mark of what might be done.

I had gotten married, and in the embrace of a more orderly life, on occasional weekends or in the evenings, I began to write again. The Korean War broke out. When I was sent over I took a small typewriter with me, thinking that if I was killed, the pages I had been writing would be a memorial. They were immature pages, to say the least. A few years later, the novel they were part of was rejected by the publishers, but one of them suggested that if I were to write another novel they would be interested in seeing it. Another novel. That might be years.

I had a journal I had kept while flying combat missions. It contained some description, but there was little shape to it. The war had the central role. One afternoon, in Florida again — I was there on temporary duty — I came back from the flight line, sat down on my cot, and began to hurriedly write out a page or so of outline that had suddenly occurred to me. It would be a novel about idealism, the true and the untrue, spare and in authentic prose. What had been missing but was missing no longer was the plot.

Why was I writing? It was not for glory; I had seen what I took to be real glory. It was not for acclaim. I knew that if the book was published, it would have to be under a pseudonym; I did not want to jeopardize a career by becoming known as a writer. I had heard the derisive references to "God-Is-My-Copilot" Scott. The ethic of fighter squadrons was drink and daring; anything else was suspect. Still, I thought of myself as more than just a pilot and imagined a book that would be in every way admirable. It would be evident that someone among the ranks of pilots had written it, an exceptional figure, unknown, but I would have the satisfaction of knowing who it was.

I wrote when I could find time. Some of the book was written at a fighter base on Long Island, the rest of it in Europe, when I was stationed in Germany. A lieutenant in my squadron who lived in the apartment adjoining ours could hear the typewriter late at night through the bedroom wall. "What are you doing," he asked one day, "writing a book?" It was meant as a joke. Nothing could be more unlikely. I was the experienced operations officer. Next step was squadron commander.

The Hunters was published by Harper and Brothers in late 1956. A section of the book appeared first in *Collier's*. Word of it spread immediately. With the rest I sat speculating as to who the writer might be, someone who had served in Korea, with the 4th Group, probably.

The reviews were good. I was thirty-two years old, the father of a child, with my wife expecting another. I had been flying fighters for seven years. I decided I had had enough. The childhood urge to write had never died, in fact, it had proven itself. I discussed it with my wife, who, with only a partial understanding of what was involved, did not attempt to change my mind. Upon leaving Europe, I resigned my commission with the aim of becoming a writer.

It was the most difficult act of my life. Latent in me, I suppose, there was always the belief that writing was greater than other things, or at least would prove to be greater in the end. Call it a delusion if you like, but within me was an insistence that whatever we did, the things that were said, the dawns, the cities, the lives, all of it had to be drawn together, made into pages, or it was in danger of not existing, of never having been. There comes a time when you realize that everything is a dream, and only those things preserved in writing have any possibility of being real.

Of the actual hard business of writing I knew very little. The first book had been a gift. I missed the active life terribly, and after a long struggle a second book was completed. It was a failure. Jean Stafford, one of the judges for a prize for which it had been routinely submitted, left the manuscript on an airplane. The book made no sense to her, she said. But there was no turning back.

A Sport and a Pastime was published six years later. It, too, did not sell. A few thousand copies, that was all. It stayed in print, however, and one by one, slowly, foreign publishers bought it. Finally, Modern Library.

The use of literature, Emerson wrote, *is to afford us a platform whence we may command a view of our present life, a purchase by which we may move it.* Perhaps this is true, but I would claim something broader. Literature is the river of civilization, its Tigris and Nile. Those who follow it, and I am inclined to say those only, pass by the glories.

Over the years I have been a writer for a succession of reasons. In the beginning, as I have said, I wrote to be admired, even if not known. Once I had decided to be a writer, I wrote hoping for acceptance, approval.

Gertrude Stein, when asked why she wrote, replied, "For praise." Lorca said he wrote to be loved. Faulkner said a writer wrote for glory. I may at times have written for those reasons, it's hard to know. Overall I write because I see the world in a certain way that no dialogue or series of them can begin to describe, that no book can fully render, though the greatest books thrill in their attempt.

A great book may be an accident, but a good one is a possibility, and it is thinking of that that one writes. In short, to achieve. The rest takes care of itself, and so much praise is given to insignificant things that there is hardly any sense in striving for it.

In the end, writing is like a prison, an island from which you will never be released but which is a kind of paradise: the solitude, the thoughts, the incredible joy of putting into words the essence of what you for the moment understand and with your whole heart want to believe.

That's What Dogs Do

AMY HEMPEL

W HY DO I WRITE? I treat this question differently today than I would have years ago, when I started to write. Then I would have said that it was an act of seduction, that sentences were "my lipstick, my lingerie, my high heels." I would have said, before I knew better, that I wrote to settle a score. In fact, the answer does not require years to change; it changes throughout the course of a single day.

Morning. Trying to train a dog is a central part of my day. So is trying to say something in a new way. But as Tom Waits said to Mark Richard about trying to make it new on another kind of keyboard, "Your hands are like dogs, going to the same places they've been." One of the tenets of successful dog training is to wait to issue a command until the dog is paying attention. If the dog is distracted, first *tune in* the dog. In Immy Humes's film *A Little Vicious*, the poet and animal trainer Vicki Hearne makes the cryptic, assured pronouncement, "You can train a dog if you've read the right poems."

There's no sport in making me blush. A stranger on the street can point to his wrist and ask for the time and I, aflame, will give it. Whether from a font of deep shame, or metabolic misfire, this response is sometimes fetching, I suppose, but more often annoying (in the seventies, when megavitamin therapy was popular, I overdosed on niacin and stayed bright red for days). Yet I don't blush when I'm with dogs, and I don't blush when I write. I take it, then, that these two activities answer a related question: Where in your life are you most yourself?

The girls' school I attended abolished its mandatory uniform the year I enrolled, but I kept the tradition alive, dressing four days out of five in navy blazer and box-pleated skirt rolled over at the waist to hike it past the dress-code length. Today, I sometimes wear that blazer over another uniform — my writing togs, sweats from the Gap, the store whose premise is, as Eve Babitz put it, "Style is no longer in style." The blazer is a reminder of the time I realized the message was not "Look at me" but "*Listen* to me."

Thus attired, I watch a TV feature on the fashion designer John Galliano. In it, a friend of his recalls the way he used to wear his clothes, in particular a shearling jacket Galliano wore upside down so that the collar was at his waist and the tail stood up to create a portrait neckline. And I thought, in a kind of simultaneous translation, I have done that, too. I have stood a story on its head and started at the end. Galliano is shown putting a leather biker jacket on a pale blond Ukrainian bride. Again, I have done that. I have dressed a delicate subject in hard, tough prose. And the reverse: described in lyrical language something ugly, something bad. Used a genteel voice to describe violence, an angry voice to take on the harmless. I mix leather and lace on the page.

WFUV not coming in, forced to listen to an oldies station. With a nod to Jeff Foxworthy, You might be a writer if . . . you gag at the Dan Hill lyric "I'm just another writer/Trapped within my truth."

Afternoon. A conversation with novelist Jim Shepard, who reminds me that we talked about this nearly twenty years ago, when we agreed that many writers shared a dissatisfaction with the normal channels of communication, a lifetime of other methods' (hand puppets!) not working very well. That, and the incentive — Hey! I took off my diaper and smeared it all over my head, and they're paying me for it!

To combat grief. Recall looking for a lost dog, calling a ranger in Maine, and the ranger's saying, "I'll look in the place I hate to look," meaning the printout of dogs found dead on the roads, and my thinking: That is my job, too, to look in the place I hate to look.

Writing is as close as I will ever come to achieving the kind of self-regard that was available to my brother at the age of ten, when he composed the shapely and authoritative English theme: "Why I Am My Favorite Person."

I once interviewed a writer who had been the college teacher of one of my literary heroes. I heard my own quest echoed as the teacher remembered this writer's early efforts: "He was a gargoyle-maker looking for a cathedral." The writer has since built enduring cathedrals that make others want to do this work, too. You want to do the thing that unglues you. You want to unglue another. In an old radio interview, James Baldwin tells Studs Terkel that what breaks the heart brilliantly about a Bessie Smith song is the way the line that follows "My house fell down" is "I can't live there no more."

I was walking home from the Latin School in Chicago after algebra class. I walked through Lincoln Park in that summer of 1968 and stopped to listen to a wild-haired man with galvanizing energy teach the "snake" method of eluding the "pigs" during a demonstration. This was days before the start of the Democratic convention, and the man was Abbie Hoffman. As I watched, Chicago police appeared and attempted to break up the meeting. I may have told friends that my eyes were stung by the tear gas the police employed. I *may* have? Of course I did. It was story-making — I'd been too far away, and that was the problem — an attempt to connect myself to history, if only from the schoolgirl sidelines.

The pleasing assonance of *macintosh, gabardine,* and *scab,* a trio of words my brothers and I made each other chant as little kids, words that — go figure — always inspired mirth.

A dog owner asks in exasperation, "Why does my dog *do* that?" And the trainer says, "Because he's a dog, and that's what dogs do."

Evening. Finding the proof, for myself, of Mark Doty's observation about the shaping forces of one's life "becoming the lens through which you see as opposed to the thing at which you are looking."

The poet John Rybicki wrote, "Our bodies are anchors thrown down by angels." How does one anchor the dead? With words.

Words, in the middle of the night, *are* people. *Comestible*, for example, is the late Christopher Coe, as applied to a "tasty specimen" in *Such Times*, the novel he stayed alive to finish. During his first hospital stay with AIDS, he phoned to say a man he didn't know had stopped into his room and asked if he was Catholic. When Christopher said no, the man excused himself, saying, "Have a better day." "Why can't I have a *good* day?" Christopher demanded, and the man told him he wouldn't have a good day until he got to Heaven. "You use it," Christopher said to me, "if I don't get a chance to."

Sanity isn't free.

Many years ago I worked as a crisis counselor with a volunteer organization. As part of the training, we counselors were made to do an exercise the point of which is lost to me now. We faced each other in pairs and waited for the signal to begin. "No, you can't." "Yes, I can." Back and forth, dozens of times, that was all we said to each other. One person saying, "No, you can't," and the other saying, "Yes, I can," until one of the partners broke. In no time I was blushing furiously (of course I was). I asked to change partners. The exercise enraged me. Which was probably the point: Could we hold our own in the face of this kind of recalcitrance? I was never *No-you-can't*. I was always *Yes-I-can*. You see where I'm going with this.

Crop circles have long held my attention. This phenomenon, which was first seen in the English Downs and later spread to the American Midwest, features large circular patterns — intersecting or contiguous perfect circles — that appear overnight in fields of wheat or oats. The success of these designs can be seen only from above, from a plane, say, flying over the field. Are crop circles supernatural imprints, or the work of human hoaxers? Night-vision cameras set up in fields in an attempt to explain the phenomenon have recorded no activity, though in the morning there have appeared immense and elaborate circles. In England, at least, folks have confessed to sneaking into fields to effect these transformations, but I was happier when they remained a mystery. I think *writing* is like swinging a scythe in the dark and finding in the morning, if you're lucky and looking from the right angle, a mysterious, well-formed pattern has emerged.

I could claim any number of highflown reasons for writing, just as you can explain certain dog behavior as submission to the alpha, or even a moral choice. But maybe it's that they're dogs, and that's what dogs do.

Stories

PAT CONROY

First, my credo.

A novel is the greatest act of passion and intellect, carpentry and largess, that a human being can pull off in one lifetime. From the very beginning, I wrote to explain my own life to myself, and I invited any readers who chose to make the journey with me to join me on the high wire. I would work without a net and without the noise of the crowd to disturb me. The view from on high is dizzying, instructive. I do not record the world exactly as it comes to me but transform it by making it pass through a prism of fabulous stories I have collected on the way. I gather stories the way a lepidopterist hoards his chloroformed specimens of rare moths, or a sunburned entomologist admires his well-ordered bottles of Costa Rican beetles. Stories are the vessels I use to interpret the world to myself. I am often called a "storyteller" by flippant and unadmiring critics. I revel in the title. I bathe in the lotions and unguents of that sweet word.

Many modern writers abjure the power of stories in their work, banish them to the suburbs of literature, drive them out toward the lower pastures of the lesser moons, and they could not be more wrong in doing so. But please, do not let me mince words in this essay in which I offer an explanation and apologia for why I write. Fear is the major cargo that American writers must stow away when the writing life calls them into its carefully chosen ranks. I have been mortally afraid of the judgment of other writers and critics since I first lifted my proud but insecure head above the South Carolina marsh grass twenty-five years ago. Some American writers are meaner than serial killers, but far more articulate, and this is always the great surprise awaiting the young men and women who swarm to the universities, their heads buzzing with all the dazzle and freshness and humbuggery of the language itself. My great fear of being attacked or trivialized by my contemporaries made me concentrate on what I was trying to do as a writer. It forced me to draw some conclusions that were my own. Here is one: The writers who scoff at the idea of the primacy of stories either are idiots or cannot write them. Many of their novels could be used in emergency situations where barbiturates are at a premium and there has been a run on Unisom at the pharmacies. "Tell me a story" still comprise four of the most powerful words in English, words that are intimately related to the complexity of history, the origins of language, the continuity of the species, the taproot of our humanity, our singularity, and art itself. I was born into the century in which novels lost their stories, poems their rhymes, paintings their form, and music its beauty, but that does not mean I have to like that trend or go along with it. I fight against these movements with every book I write.

Good writing is the hardest form of thinking. It involves the agony of turning profoundly difficult thoughts into lucid form, then forcing them into the tight-fitting uniform of language, making them visible and clear. If the writing is good, then the result seems effortless and inevitable. But when you want to say something life-changing or ineffable in a single sentence, you face both the limitations of the sentence itself and the extent of your own talent. When you come close to succeeding, when the words pour out of you just right, you understand that these sentences are all part of a river flowing out of your own distant, hidden ranges, and all words become the dissolving snow that feeds your bright mountain streams forever. The language locks itself in the icy slopes of our own high passes, and it is up to us, the writers, to melt the glaciers within us. When these glaciers calve and break off, we get to call them novels, the changelings of our burning spirits, our lifework.

I have always taken a child's joy in the painterly loveliness of the English language. As a writer, I try to make that language pitch and roll, soar above the Eastern Flyway, reverse its field at will, howl and reel in the darkness, bellow when frightened, and pray when it approaches the eminence or divinity of nature itself. My well-used dictionaries and thesauri sing out to me when I write, and all English words are the plainsong of my many-tongued, long-winded ancestors who spoke before me. I write because I once fell in love with the sound of words as spoken by my comely, Georgia-born mother. I use the words that sound prettiest or most right to me as I drift into that bright cocoon where the writer loses himself in the silks of language. When finished, I adore the way the words look back at me after I have written them down on long yellow legal sheets. They are written in my hand, and their imperfect shapes thrill me. I can feed on the nectar of each work I write, and some are salt-rimed with the storm-flung Atlantic on them, some mountain-born, writhing in laurel, but each with a dark taste of my own life fresh upon it. What richer way to meet the sunlight than bathing each day of my life in my island-born language, the one that Shakespeare breathed on, Milton wrestled with, Jane Austen tamed, and Churchill rallied the squadrons of England with? I want to use the whole English language as the centerpiece of a grand alliance or concordance with my work. I see myself as its acolyte, its spy in the college of cardinals, its army in the field. I try to turn each sentence into a bright container made of precious metals and glittering glass. It is the carrier and aqueduct of the sweetest elixir of English words themselves. I build these sentences slowly. Like a glassblower, I use air and fire to shape the liquids as they form in my imagination. I long for that special moment when I take off into the pure, oxygen-rich sky of a sentence that streaks off into a night where I cannot follow, where I lose control, when the language seizes me and shakes me in such a way that I feel like both its victim and its copilot.

Story and language brought me to the craft of writing, then passion and my childhood provided both the structure and the details. When I was busy growing up on the Marine bases of my youth, my mother cast a spell on me that I found all but unbreakable. Peg Conroy was rough-born and southern-shaped, and I heard the stories of her Depression childhood so often that I have never been able to throw off the belief that I've known poverty inside and out from a very early age. Each night of my boyhood, my mother read to me, and I still hear her voice, lovely beneath soft lamplight, whenever I sit down with a pen in my hand. It was my mother who told me she was raising me to be a "southern writer," though I have never been sure that she knew what that meant. My sister Carol Conroy listened to that same voice and heard those same stories, and her book of poetry, *The Beauty Wars*, was published by Norton in 1991. Part of my childhood that is most vivid to me was being chief witness to the shaping of an American poet in the bedroom next to mine. My sister and I grew up stung by the consequence of language in my mother's house.

My father, the Chicago-born Donald Conroy, brought the sensibilities of Augie March and Studs Lonigan to the cockpits of the fighter planes he flew over target areas along the coastal South. My father was a pure man of action; he thought books made handsome furniture, but I never saw him read one. The strongest Marine I ever knew raised me up to manhood in a house that had the feel of a gulag to it. When I first read *The Iliad* in high school, I had no problem placing my father in the midst of those glittering spearmen who sat by their confreres in the shadows of poor, besieged Troy. When I wrote *The Great Santini*, I learned things about my father's military career that took me by surprise and have made me proud to this very day. Although I still believe he was a bad father to his seven children, I should like to think that my country was a far safer place because men such as my father patrolled the American skies. You would not have liked to be an enemy soldier when Don Conroy lowered his flaps and caught you moving across his field of vision with his Corsair loaded with napalm.

I was born a warrior's son, and this is a vital piece of evidence in my biography. My father treated his children like an unruly platoon that took overly long to shape up. He raised me to be a fighter pilot like himself, and that is what I had planned to do before I was waylaid by literature. Yet my books have the feel of some invisible though embattled country, where the field artillery is always exchanging rounds between chapters. Like all battlefields, my novels fill up with smoke and noise and the screams of the wounded and the answering calls of medics low-crawling through the blasted, cratered fields with their canteens and their morphine ready. My father taught me the way of the warrior at the same time my mother was turning me into a wordsmith.

War itself was a fundamental reality in my household, and my father was called to battle the way other fathers were called to distant cities for sales conferences. Civilian fathers sold shoes or life insurance while my father wiped out battalions of North Korean regulars by setting them on fire. As a father, Don Conroy carried a few shortcomings into the task of fathering, and I never thought he could tell the real difference between a sortie against the enemy and a family picnic. My parents taught me everything I needed to know about the dangers and attractions of the extreme. Even today, the purely outrageous to me feels completely natural. My novels reflect the absurdity and the exorbitance of a house in which the fully unexpected was our daily bread. My father once wiped out a dozen tanks working their way toward Marine lines in Korea, and my mother's hobby was collecting poisonous snakes. It is not my fault I was raised by Zeus and Hera, but my books mirror the odd, hothouse environment of my astonished childhood. All writers are both devotees and prisoners of their childhoods, and of the images that accrued during those early days on earth when each of us played out the mystery of Adam and Eve in our own way. My mother's voice and my father's fists are the two bookends of my childhood, and they form the basis of my art.

My parents taught me many of the exigencies and pitfalls of character. My father seemed prehistoric in his simplicity, a one-celled carnivore with a violent, unpredictable temper. Living with him was like being perched in a village near Vesuvius. He made life seem dangerous, but he made me alert and vigilant, and he wore the city of Chicago like a bad tattoo on his character. I still watch my back when I enter the Chicago city limits.

We seemed to move every year, but the South was carry-on luggage with my mother. She hailed from a testy, improvident South. The Battle of Atlanta was actually fought along the grounds where I was born and along the road where my mother brought me home to my grandmother's house on Rosedale Road. From my earliest days, my mother taught me to hate with all my heart William Tecumseh Sherman, the leader of the invasion force that had left the South bleeding and prostrate as he cut his wake across a bereft, helpless land. Many years passed before I began to realize that it was my father, not Sherman, whom my mother had been talking about. Peg Conroy thought she was teaching me history when in fact she was delivering my first instruction in metaphor.

If my father's birthplace had been rural Georgia, and my mother had come up in South Chicago, I am positive that I would be known as a writer out of the Chicago School this very day. My mother was multiformed, hydra-headed, an untamable shapeshifter whose love of miscellany was a kind of genius. The women in my books all share an air of mystery, an unwinnable allure that I trace back to my inability to figure out what made my mother tick. When I try to pin down my mother's soft, armor-covered spirit, when I fix it on a slide beneath a microscope, I can feel it all becoming immaterial before my steady gaze. The colors rearrange themselves and the cosmetology of her womanhood reverses itself. My hunt will always be for my mother. She could not give me herself, but she gave me literature as a replacement. I have no idea who she was, and I write my books as a way of find-ing out.

Although I was trained in the way of the Marine Corps and brought to manhood in the backwater South, my mother had pos-session of the keys to the kingdom of art. She turned me into an insatiable, fanatical reader. It was her gentle urging, her hurt, in-sistent voice, that led me to discover my identity by taking a work-ing knowledge of the great books with me always. She wanted me to read everything of value, and we looked like bibliophiles or book thieves when our family returned from libraries during my youth. My mother taught me to outread my entire generation, as she had done hers. I believe, and I think fairly, that I have done that — that I have not only outread my own generation of writers but outread them in such a way that whole secret libraries sepa-rate us. I started this solitary voyage in high school, thinking it would give me an advantage over every single rival when I later began the strange business of writing novels. I have tried to read two hundred pages every day of my life since I was a freshman in high school because I knew that I would come to the writing of books without the weight of culture and learning that a well-established, confidently placed family could offer its children. I collected those long, melancholy lists of the great books that high school English teachers passed out to college-bound students, and I relied on having consumed those serious litanies of books as a way to ease my way into the literary life.

Even today, I hunt for the fabulous books that will change me utterly and for all time. Great writing sticks to your soul the way beggar's lice adheres to your pants cuffs after a walk through un-tended fields. I find myself happiest in the middle of a book in which I forget that I am reading, but am instead immersed in a made-up life lived at the highest pitch. Reading is the most rewarding form of exile and the most necessary discipline for novelists who burn with the ambition to get better.

Here is what I want from a book, what I demand, what I pray for when I take up a novel and begin to read the first sentence: I want everything and nothing less, the full measure of a writer's heart. I want a novel so poetic that I do not have to turn to the standby anthologies of poetry to satisfy that itch for music, for perfection and economy of phrasing, for exactness of tone. Then, too, I want a book so filled with story and character that I read page after page without thinking of food or drink because a writer has possessed me, crazed me with an unappeasable thirst to know what happens next. Again, I know that story is suspect in the high precincts of American fiction, but only because it brings entertainment and pleasure, the same responses that have always driven puritanical spirits at the dinner table wild when the talk turns to sexual intercourse and incontinence.

When an author sets the table right, there will be no need to pass either the foie gras or the barbecue because the characters will grab me by the collar. They will spring to life so fully developed, so richly contained in the oneness of their own universe, that they will populate the cafés and verandahs and alleyways of a city I will never want to leave. Few things linger longer or become more indwelling than that feeling of both completion and emptiness when a great book ends. That the book accompanies the reader forever, from that day forward, is part of literature's profligate generosity.

All through my life I have told myself — no, ordered myself — to read more deeply, read everything of consequence, let the words of some new writer settle like the dust of silica into the ledges and sills of my consciousness. When I find myself engaged in the reading of some magical, surprising book, I ask myself these questions: Can I match this depth? Can I incorporate this splendid work, ingest it whole into my bloodstream, where it can become part of my thinking and dreaming life? What can this writer do that I can't? Can I steal the genius of this writer and learn all of the unappropriated lessons, then turn them into something astonishing that flows out of me because I was moved by the originality and courage and eloquence of another writer? Very early on, I set up for myself the endless task of reading and incorporating books of large and exuberant vision. By reading these luminous works, I learn the shy secrets of my craft, but I also gain some idea of the novel's fertility, its free-flowing immensity. In the middle of reading a life-changing book, I feel like that grain of sand, that famous irritation in the tissue of a healthy oyster, and I can feel the pearl beginning to form around me. I welcome the silvering, then the hardening as I ingest the sheer beauty of another writer's language. I let myself be taken by, then lost in, the maze and wizardry of a gift not my own. I allow the subsuming to take place, then the transfiguration. I await the aura of wealth and mother-of-pearl handed over to the passionate reader. It is communion, and it is religious in nature. I ask a great deal of a book: astonishment, transformation, art, and nothing less. When I write a book, I move with all the magic of language toward a fixed star, offering a present of my troubled, violent spirit, and I wish to leave the reader with everything.

When I first sat down to write these books, I had to teach myself how to go about it. I called upon that regiment of beloved writers, living and dead, who had written the books that had changed the way I looked at myself and the world. I promised myself that each novel would seem like a world unto itself. I wanted a specific gravity, changeable weather, a real geography that could provide a starting point for a mapmaker's art. I wanted the atmosphere of the novels to feel like the one I had breathed in as a boy when I found myself in the grip of a mother-haunted imagination to which I owed both fealty and homage. I demanded living trees with actual names, flowers growing in their proper seasons, characters who spoke their minds, who lived as free men and women outside of my jurisdiction. My city of made-up people would live their own complex lives without my permission or my intrusion into their own sovereignty. I wanted my fictional world to feel like the one I had grown up in, with no whitewashing of the horror that stood in the doorway of any given human moment. All my rivers had to be clean enough for the cobia, the herring, and the shad to swim upstream to spawn, because I was going back to my own sources to find the secrets of the world. I desired to be one of those writers who always followed the creek bed to that source, that clear pool where the mother's roe floated in still water above the glittering pebbles.

Nothing lazy would ever enter my books. I try to write down every word with caution and a sense of craft, as though I were carving hieroglyphics on the tomb of a well-loved king. Writing is both hard labor and one of the most pleasant forms that fanaticism can take. I take infinite care in how a sentence sounds to me. I rise out of the oral tradition of the American South, and words have to sound a certain way if they're to come out right.

In my first years, my identity as a writer was drawn toward amplitude, fullness, and extravagance. I worshiped those writers who made me feel sated, coddled, spoiled with all the excess that too much attention and love can provide. The overreachers called out my name, and I responded with great zeal. I longed for writers to take me to the absolute crests and limits of their talents, but

I did not want them to leave out the grand tours of the abysses and spiritual Death Valleys they encountered along the way.

But since I have tried to read everything, I have also found myself falling for the seductiveness of economy, the telling of a story with swiftness, velocity, and even severity. Exactness is a virtue in even the most word-possessed writer. There is enormous power in stating something simply and well. Action sequences always require the straight line in the presentation, the most solid, sequential phrases, and the punchiest, most telling Anglo-Saxon sentences. Action brims and stirs. There is delicacy, craft, and restraint in all this, as in the making of a dry martini. But sometimes a lot more is required. Then you must go inside yourself to find the lift-off into the dark side of language's many rooms. When you have made a new sentence, or even an image that works well, it is a palace where language itself has lit a new lamp. It is why a writer sits alone, fingering memory and shaping imagination during all the lost, solitary days.

As a writer, I have tried to make and remake myself over and over again. I try to notice everything, and if I take the time to write it, I would simply like to write it better than anyone else possibly could. If I am describing the Atlantic Ocean, I want to make that portion of the high seas mine forevermore, and I do not want the reader daydreaming about Herman Melville's ocean while getting a suntan on poor Conroy's. I try to be athletic and supple with my talent. I train it, urge it on, drive it to exceed itself, knowing in my bones that I need to be watchful about slippage, weariness, and running on empty. The safe writers have never interested me, do not excite a single shiver of curiosity within me. I can read five pages and know I am in the hands of a writer whose feet are yawningly and cunningly placed on safe ground. Safety is a crime writers should never commit unless they are after tenure or praise. A novelist must wrestle with all the mysteries and strangeness of life itself, and anyone who does not wish to accept that grand, bone-chilling commission should write book reviews, editorials, or health-insurance policies instead. The idea of a novel should stir your blood, and you should rise to it like a lion lifting up at the smell of impala. It should be instinctual, incurable, unanswerable, and a calling, not a choice.

I came to the writing life because my father's warplanes took off against me, and my mother's hurt South longed for her special voice. Nothing is more difficult for a writer to overcome than a childhood of privilege, but this was never a concern of mine. To experience a love that is too eloquent sometimes makes for a writer without edges or karats or facets. I have drawn long and often from the memory book of my youth, the local and secret depository where my central agony cowers in the limestone cave, licking its wounds, awaiting my discovery of it. Art is one of the few places where talent and madness can actually go to squirrel away inside each other.

I have used my books as instruments to force my way into the world. It was with surprise and wonder that I discovered that the same elemental, dangerous chemistry that moves through the volcanoes of the earth also moved through me. Through words, I learned that life and art can be raised to a fever pitch, to sacramental levels, that ecstasy itself is within easy reach for all of us, but the secret is in knowing it is there and when to reach for it. I want always to be writing the book I was born to write. A novel is my fingerprint, my identity card, and the writing of novels is one of the few ways I have found to approach the altar of God and creation itself. You try to worship God by performing the singularly courageous and impossible favor of knowing yourself. You watch for the black wings of fighters writing messages in the skies over the South. Your mother plays with snakes and poison and raises you to tell the stories that will make all our lives clear. It all congeals and moves and hurts in the remembering.

I can ask for nothing more.

Writing and a Life Lived Well

Notes on Allan Gurganus

ANN PATCHETT

THERE ARE MAYBE TWENTY different stories and all of them are true.

I write because as a child I had such a hard time making my letters, remembering which direction the S was supposed to face. I had a painful time with spelling, punctuation, wicked contractions. I sat at my tiny desk at six and seven and eight and made nearly indecipherable marks, fishhooks and barbed wire. I was one of those kids. I struggled. I lost things. When papers were finished, they were crumpled into coat pockets. I was so poor at the form of writing, the physical act of pencil to paper, that I knew instinctively the secret to survival was in the content. Be funny, be clever, and you will scrape by. Cleverness, once learned, can be the stairs that take you down to more interesting places.

The nun who collected those papers, who tortured me for my stupidity, I write for her. Even as a child I wanted to write for revenge, to show them all, but especially this particular nun, that I had been misjudged.

A story that must be told quickly to avoid melodrama involves an especially bad car accident my sister and I were in. I remember waking up in a hospital, eight years old (this is true), and thinking, Now I can be anything, so I'll be a writer.

"And the life I live now's an extra life," Frost said, "I can waste as I please. . . ."

I write because I think my mother should have been a writer. She wrote wonderful poems. I write because my father lived on the other side of the country when I was growing up, and we wrote long letters to each other. He missed us and we missed him terribly. I made a habit of storing up my life and writing it down for him. I write because of my father's strong, clear handwriting.

There is more, but any of these reasons is enough. I said it to whoever asked, "Ann, what do you want to be?" I felt like I was picking my answer out of the air, but it was always the same answer. I always and only wanted to be a writer. I have often wondered whether, if I had said "a fireman," or "an opera singer," I would have then barreled toward those professions with such complete single-mindedness.

If there had been a supportive nun and naturally good penmanship, if there had been enough money for my father to call more often and therefore he never wrote to me, would I write? I wrote after school, during school. While my girlfriends danced and dated, I sat and wrote. Every ounce of gangly energy I had went onto paper. I sprawled. I mass-produced.

I went to college and took a writing class, and the next year I took another one.

It was in that class, the second one, that everything changed. Now we go from maybe twenty possible reasons why I became a writer to the one certain, definite reason: I write because Allan Gurganus taught me to.

Sixteen years ago, Allan was thirty-four, the age I am now. I like to say I knew Allan Gurganus before he was Allan Gurganus. This was long before *Oldest Living Confederate Widow Tells All*. He wasn't famous to the general public yet, but at Sarah Lawrence, in Westchester County, and, I imagine, in most of Manhattan, he was famous. He moved in an unmistakable cloud of celebrity. He had what must have been the best office on campus, with a fireplace and French glass doors leading out onto a garden, which in the spring was full of heavy French tulips and dogwood trees. He wore linen trousers in the spring. The chairs beside his desk were deep and dark and full of pillows. There were copies of Chekhov and a framed black-and-white picture of John Cheever. There were drawings he had done, postcards from exotic friends in equally exotic places, a large crazy quilt on the wall made out of satins and velvet. When he walked into a room, we stirred, we leaned toward him. Everybody did. Allan, young, with a handful of well-published stories, was as dazzling to us as Chekhov or Cheever themselves would have been.

How he looked (wonderful), his impeccable taste, how people spoke to him and spoke of him, have nothing to do with writing, but everything to do with my being a writer. No one made a better impression than Allan, and as I was eighteen at the time, an age when one is most susceptible to appearances, I was deeply moved. This was what it would be like to be a writer, this was how it would look. Yes. Heaven. Sign me up. Our text for the class was the collected stories of Isaac Babel, which are still here on my desk.

The class, a weekly fiction workshop that lasted two semesters, had fourteen people in it. I remember each of them. I remember their stories in a way I cannot remember stories from any other class I have taken or taught since. The deal was as follows: we were to write a story a week, every week, until it was over. For a while there were assignments, the most skeletal nudges toward plot: write a story about an animal; write a fairy tale; write a story from the point of view of . . . and so forth. Then even those little starters fell away and we were out there alone, typing. I am respectful of people whose college careers consisted of classes I was (am) unfit to audit — inorganic chemistry, advanced statistics, upper-level Greek — but I would say the best of them would have struggled under this particular load. Ninety percent of what I know about fiction writing I learned that year. Write it out. Tell the truth. Stack up the pages. Learn to write by writing. Slowing down was for later, years later. Learn the sea by sailing it. We were not writing for keeps, we were writing out our mistakes, finding our strengths by stumbling over them in the dark. We were to keep going at all costs. To miss a week was to have two stories due, which was a little like taking in a mouthful of water when you were doing your best not to drown.

At eighteen, I had already spent a good ten years dreaming about the job I wanted. I came to Allan's class with no small amount of motivation, ambition, not for fame but for real ability. What I lacked was skill. I had no habits, and writers are people who desperately need habits to fill up their days. Allan's habits were based in vast quantities of reading and writing, reading and rewriting. He was somewhere between Balanchine and Cus D'Amato. We danced until our feet bled, punched until we could no longer bob or weave. He would call us "Dearest" and "My Angel," but the standards didn't bend to meet our needs. He seemed to expect of us what he expected of himself.

Although it never occurred to me at the time, I have wondered in every class I have since taught, What must he have been thinking of, assigning so much work? Every week a maelstrom of stories, and he responded to each generously in brown fountain pen, giving nuts-and-bolts advice of the kind you'd never get from an editor, about how to actually make a story better. There was an enormous generosity in him. I don't have children, but I believe that people parent in response to their own parents, being either like them or as unlike them as possible. When I teach, it is in response to Allan's teaching. I try to find that level of generosity within myself, and never come close. He took us on a field trip to the Cloisters. He had a black-and-white class portrait taken for which he wore a dark, double-breasted blazer. He read to us. It was the first time I heard Raymond Carver's "Shall We Dance." The first time I heard anything of *Lolita*. One week he read to us from a book of conversations with Joan Crawford, how she sat at her kitchen table and wept over a failed dinner party. Sometimes he read us stories of his own. Those were the moments I remember most vividly. I remember long passages of things he read that I never saw again. Why do I write? Because the person I wanted to be came down and sat with us from time to time and showed us what he was working on, as if to say that what we were doing was all the same thing.

Allan and I have been in irregular touch over the years, but we are not friends. Allan is my teacher and I am his student, and no amount of time will change that. I send him Christmas cards. He has written me letters of recommendation. When I sold my first story to the *Paris Review*, he sent me two dozen white roses, which meant more than the publication itself. I have never written to please Allan. I'm not entirely sure if he's read my books or liked them. I mail him copies just the same. I do not wish to write like

Allan, though I greatly admire his work. He never taught us to mimic. I recognize the fact that he has had hundreds of students, some of them very successful, most of whom would have been glad to write this essay. Mentors are extremely hard to come by. The ones who are generous might not really have anything to teach you. The ones who are brilliant often prefer to keep their brilliance to themselves. To have received some genuine guidance in my life, to have received it at a time when I was capable of listening in a way I probably no longer am, was a great gift. In the end, the lesson retold in its most basic form was this: write with great truthfulness; work harder than you thought possible; have passion, enormous, sweeping passion. Give it first to your work. Let your work have all of the passion it requires, and whatever is left, put into your life. What is left varies greatly for me from year to year.

Writing, for me, is bound up completely in my quality of life. There is much about writing a novel that weighs me down, as if I am having to live two lives, my own and the one I create. But in writing I have purpose, I'm doing the thing I was meant to do. When I'm not writing — and I can go for long stretches without it — things are easier. But this life lived only for myself takes on a certain lightness that I find almost unbearable after a while, as if everything has become a moderately entertaining sitcom.

Last summer I was driving to Cape Cod and stopped off in North Carolina for a wedding. I called Allan and told him I would be passing through the town where he lived and hoped that I could see him. He said that he was leaving for Paris, but that he wanted me to come and spend the night in his house anyway. "I'd love to think of you here," he said.

And so I went. It is a very small town, and he was sitting on the front porch when I arrived. For Allan, there is still a great deal of passion left over after he has given his work everything it requires. There is passion for his friends, for his rambling gardens, and for his house, which is very much like a novel itself and would take a novel's number of pages to describe with any sort of justice. We sat in his kitchen for an hour before it was time for me to drive him to the airport in Raleigh. We talked about business and books and people we both remembered. He recounted the plot of the story I had written as a submission to get into his class sixteen years before. As far as I know, he is the only person who ever saw it. I never worked on it again and threw my copy away. "I liked that story," he said. "I knew when I read it that you'd do well."

How could he remember? What had he seen? When I came back to his house, I was glad to be alone. I could wander around the house and study the murals he had painted on the walls, soldiers with mighty horses on the second floor, Pompeii in the downstairs front room. It took me half the night just to look at his books. It took me all of the morning before I left to take in the garden.

I went back to his house again that same summer. I was in North Carolina for the filming of a movie and was invited to Allan's fiftieth-birthday party. It was the kind of party I had often imagined but had never actually seen. All of the women and some of the men came in wide-brimmed hats and danced barefoot in the grass when the jazz combo played. There were candles in the trees. There were testimonials. Allan moved among us, covering his own lawn in circles, telling jokes, taking everyone's hand. Each guest was made to feel that he or she was his secret favorite, the one he was most delighted to see. These were not students, for the most part, not people he had taught to write, but they were people whose feelings for him were not dissimilar to my own. We had all learned something from Allan, the expansiveness of his life, the reckless generosity. When it was dark, there was still champagne and then there were fireworks. Most of the guests had gone home by the time my friend Lynn Roth and I went to find him to say good-bye. Lynn had come with me; she was a screenwriter for the film. She had never met Allan before. When he walked us to the door, she told him that he had the most remarkable quality of life she had ever seen.

"And, my dear," he said, taking her hand, "I never for a moment imagined that it would be any other way."

Let me add this to the list: in my mind, sixteen years ago, Allan Gurganus made the distinct and permanent association between writing and a life lived well, a life that would stand for compassion, generosity, and grace. I do not mean to say there is no suffering; everyone knows about that. There is suffering in every life. There is more, perhaps, when it is your business to see it. But there can also be great beauty. If that's the way you want to play the cards, all of the struggle and loneliness of the job can be made into joy. We chose this, after all, we write because we wanted to do it more than anything else, and even when we hate it, there is nothing better.

Easing My Heart Inside

TERRY MCMILLAN

I NEVER WANTED TO BE A WRITER. As a kid, all I ever dreamed of was living in a house with central air and heat and a toilet that flushed. My mother *told* me I was going to college — no ifs, ands, or buts about it — and that I need not be concerned with "having anybody's babies" until after I had a degree in my hand. As a result, I was too scared to have sex during high school, when all my friends were having it, so I took to reading instead. Got my first job shelving books at our local library and spent many $1.25-per-hour hours hiding in the 700 and 900 sections.

This is where my dreams began to turn outward. I started traveling all over the world. I flew with Amelia Earhart. Sat with the Brontës. Rode in a sleigh in the snow with Robert Frost. Touched and smelled green with Thoreau. John Steinbeck fooled me with that story that wasn't really about mice: I thought he could've been black. James Baldwin frightened me when I saw his dark face on his book jacket: When did black people start writing books? I wondered. And then there was *Bartlett's Quotations,* which blew my young mind because it was like this dictionary of thought on all kinds of topics that I used to lie awake at night and ponder but never had anybody to talk to about. I didn't know then that I was already lonely. I couldn't share my feelings, and I knew no one really cared what I felt or thought.

But then I went to college, and my reading became a little broader, and one day this guy whose name I still can't remember broke a major portion of my heart and I found myself sitting on my twin-size bed in this tiny college apartment and I was in a coma for like four hours because I was unable to move (although I didn't try) and finally when I felt the blood flowing through my body again something hit my brain and exploded and I jumped up without knowing where I was going or what I was about to do and I grabbed a pen and a steno pad and began to write these words down one two three ten at a time and I wasn't even thinking about what I was doing because it happened so fast and I didn't realize until I was out of breath and four whole pages were filled with these words and I exhaled a deep sigh of relief and exhaustion but I suddenly felt better but then I panicked because when I looked at these words it sounded and looked like a poem and I knew damn well I didn't write this shit because I had never written anything before in my life.

And that's how it started.

This writing stuff saved me. It has become my way of responding to and dealing with things I find too disturbing or distressing or painful to handle in any other way. It's safe. Writing is my shelter. I don't hide behind the words; I use them to dig inside my heart to find the truth. I guess I can say, honestly, that writing also offers me a kind of patience I don't have in my ordinary day-to-day life. It makes me stop. It makes me take note. It affords me a kind of sanctuary that I can't get in my hurried and full-to-the-brim-with-activity life.

Besides that, I'm selfish. And self-absorbed. But I've discovered that writing makes me less so. It has made me more compassionate. In fact, that's what I've always prayed for: to have more compassion. For everybody. I've learned that every human being has feelings, despite the fact that sometimes I have my doubts and people think no one understands how they feel and that no one could possibly feel the same way. It's simply not true. Shock shock shock.

I'm also nosy. And I want to understand why I do some of the things I do and why we're so stupid, and in order to come close to empathizing I had to learn how to get under someone else's skin. Writing has become my *under*.

If I understood half of what I did or felt, I probably wouldn't waste my time writing. But I like the probing. I like being scared sometimes. I like worrying about the folks I write about. I want to know if everything's gonna turn out OK for them. I want to show what can happen when we err, and when we "do the right thing," because as they say, no matter what you do, sometimes, "shit happens." I like how we handle the shit when it does hit the fan. Especially when we throw it in the blades ourselves.

I just want to pay attention. To the details of everyday life. I want to be a better person. I want to feel good more often. I want to know, when I don't, *why* I don't. Writing gives me this.

Chekhov said, "Man will become better only when you make him see what he is like." This is what I'm trying to do when I portray African-American men and women behaving "badly." I'm not trying to "air dirty laundry"; I'm just trying to get us to hold up a mirror and take a long look. Most of us don't think about what we do, we just act and react. Many of us don't reflect or wonder what larger issues are really at stake in our lives.

Writing is helping me mature. As long as I'm not bullshitting myself, the act itself forces me to face and understand my flaws and weaknesses and strengths, and if I'm honest — really fucking honest — then writing is like a wake-up call. I become my own therapist. Because nobody knows me better than me, and if I do my job, I can ease my heart inside another character's until I feel what he or she feels and think the way he or she thinks. When I'm able to become, say, a chronic liar — using lies as a way to defend myself — then I know I'm on the right track because I can write about someone whom I do not in real life respect or admire but whom I've come to understand. Writing has taught me not to be so judgmental. I usually write about people I don't necessarily favor, who do things I would never dream of doing, and therefore I sort of have to make myself undo my own sense of thinking and being. It can be exhilarating, freeing, a real eye-opener, and painful as hell.

Maybe I'm weird, but I want to know what it feels like to die. To have your heart broken. Why people hurt each other intentionally. Why folks lie. And cheat. What kind of person can kill another person and sleep at night? What does a man feel when he beats his wife? How does she stay with him? How do children learn to hate? What is a good parent? What's it feel like to discover that you are gay when you're twelve? Why do some people not have the capacity to forgive? How long can I hold a grudge? And why are some people nicer and more likable, more responsible than others?

I could go on and on. But the bottom line is that I didn't make a conscious decision to become a writer. I never did it for the money. I never did it for fame. Who knew? Who ever knows? I think somehow the craft chose me. The words have given me ownership and a sense of security. Writing is the only place I can be myself and not feel judged. And I like it there.

Why the Daily Writing of Fiction Matters

RICK BASS

I LIVE IN A REMOTE VALLEY deep in the woods, and I must confess that when I go into town and encounter someone who asks where I live and what I do, for the longest time it was not entirely with pride that I would tell him or her I was a writer, and a thing I especially did not enjoy admitting was that I was a fiction writer. It seemed to me to be like answering, "Oh, I breathe," or "I'm a yawner," or "I look at air a lot." Hunch-shouldered over a one-dimensional sheet of paper, scowling and frowning at the patterns of ink, sometimes laughing, I might as well have answered, it seemed to me then, "I'm invisible" or "I don't do anything."

For a long time there was a shadow to my movements, and to my life, that asked, How real is this thing that I do? Writing was invisible and airy enough, vaporous an act as it was — one trafficked in ideas as one might traffic in smoke, or scent, or memory — but then even worse, it seemed, was the writing of fiction:

74

invisible ideas about things that had never even happened. A layer of the invisible laid crossways on another layer of the invisible: a grid, a subworld, of nothing. The black hole into which one disappeared for three, four, five hours a day, where everything was within arm's reach and where it all moved very slowly. Even in those rare moments when the pen raced full tilt across the page, left to right, the hand took roughly ten to fifteen seconds to traverse that eight-inch span.

It's such a slow world down there — the invisible second basement below the invisible first basement — that when you emerge, blinking and pulse-stilled, later in the day, and walk up the path from your writing cabin to your real life in your real house, even the most mundane movements of the earth seem to split your mind with onrushing speed. Simple conversation, thought, numerical gymnastics, even a seemingly easy task such as making a phone call or peeling a potato — anything of the regular nature of the world conspires to race past you like a Roger Clemens fastball; you open your mouth to respond, you raise your hand, but by that point the world has moved again. The electric sight of a butterfly dancing over tall green grass causes your brow to furrow, and you watch it with a thing like exhaustion. Things were so slow and controlled just a few minutes ago, back in your writing! Very carefully, then, you begin to ease back into humanity. You walk carefully, as if on ice, disbelieving, perhaps, if your immersion or submersion has been deep enough, that this is the real world, or rather, that you have any business in it.

You make a conscious commitment to try to enjoy the physicality of that part of the day that's left. You can't help but think (even if only with your body, like a kind of echo) about the world you're trying to remake, or protect, or attack, or celebrate — the one you left behind. And when you have a good day, a good *phys-*

ical day, in that second part of the day, you sometimes feel like a traitor when you encounter joy or pleasure, or anything else deeply felt.

Which brings me, I think, to the reason writing is important (the reason any kind of art is important), and especially fiction writing. Art is an engagement of the senses; art sharpens the acuity with which emotions, and the other senses, are felt or imagined (and again, here, it challenges reality: What is the difference between feeling happy and really *being* happy? What is the difference between imagining you can taste something and really tasting it? A hair's breadth; a measurement less than the thickness of a dried work-skein of ink on paper).

The reading of good writing can engage the senses, can stretch them and keep them alive in the world — that is, sensate, rather than numb. Above all, in the reading of good fiction, the reader is called upon not only to believe in the thing being described, but to feel it deeply even while knowing full well on some conscious level going in that *it ain't true*— that it's made up. This is a double stretching, one that can require of the reader's mind an extraordinary suppleness. I think that almost everyone would posit that this is a good thing. To put it bluntly, I remember a football coach's arguing with some players whom he wanted to begin lifting weights. They were afraid of becoming muscle-bound and losing their speed and flexibility. The coach was desperate, spitting flecks of saliva in his inarticulate rage. Finally he understood how to explain it: "It'll make you faster and *more* flexible," he said. "You can stretch muscle. You can't stretch fat."

Fiction, by its very nature — being about a thing that, at best, at its most realistic, has not quite happened that way *yet* — is about a stretching and widening of borders, about options and possibilities of energy and character. Near a story's end, of course, as in life, all this possibility funnels into only one seemingly foregone, inescapable conclusion, but in the beginning, anything is possible — anything can be woven out of the elements at hand.

Good fiction, to my mind, breathes possibility, which is to say also that it breathes a kind of diversity, into every assemblage of characters, energies, and ideas. Reading it makes our minds supple, able to go two ways with equal strength rather than just one way: to consider the "real" but also equally to consider and feel the life of the story we're reading.

Fiction has always mattered because of its ability, its mandate, to reach across the borders and boundaries of reality, to give one the feeling, with each paragraph read, of new territory — but if you believe, as I do, that despite the stitchwork lacing of fiber-optic cables and such, the world is becoming more fragmented and more brittle, then anything that retains the ability to leap across those ever-encroaching and constricting borders is only going to become more important, particularly as we, the hungry, benumbed mass of us, continue swelling at the seams, funneling toward a conclusion that has felt inevitable all along: what my liberal friends call a loss of cultural diversity and what my right-wing friends (way right) call "one world order."

My beloved valley — the Yaak Valley of extreme northwestern Montana — is but a perfect example of and metaphor for every other finely crafted and specific system that is breaking down or being swallowed whole and assimilated, made general (and hence weak). The Yaak is the wildest place I've ever seen — ice-carved twelve thousand years ago into a magic little seam between the Pacific Northwest and the northern Rockies. It's a land a writer could love easily, a showcase of giant predators — grizzly bears, black bears, wolves, wolverines, golden eagles, coyotes, bald eagles, mountain lions, lynx, owls, bobcats — consuming big prey such as moose, deer, elk, even caribou.

Almost everything eats something else up here: so much tooth-and-claw, so much tension and remaking, so much chase and pursuit — so much like a writer stalking and following a story. Even the insects in the old-growth forests up here are largely carnivorous, consuming each other rather than preying on the forest itself, in which case they would devour the very thing that gives them nourishment.

If the forest in the Yaak, with its seething, *specific* characters, its incredible richness of diversity, and hence possibility, is so very much like the mind of a fiction writer, then understand, too, that the politics and human influences on the valley, the corporate designs on it, are also so very much like the mind of generalized, homogeneous, world-merge society. You do not need to be a scientist — or a reader or writer of fiction — to take a walk in the Yaak and know that, beautiful and mysterious though it is (seething with mosquitoes and black flies and steamy summer rain), the forest stands at the edge of some kind of loss.

Giant square and rectangular and triangular clearcuts are carved out of the valley yearly, stamped onto the sides of the steep mountains, baking and drying to arid lifeless moonscapes, on land that was previously a rich, diverse jungle. Roads rip through these old, secret corridors, old, secret paths of wolves and grizzlies, bringing light and heat into a place that was previously cool and dark.

Everything in the Yaak is being cut off from every other thing. The roads and clearcuts reduce the living, pulsing whole into a series of isolated, machinelike parts. William Kittredge has said, "As we destroy that which is natural, we eat ourselves alive."

In the face of such loss, such pain, one can enter shock. Numbness becomes a defensive mechanism, as does denial.

Fiction can be like a salve or balm to reverse this encrustation. Like sweating on a good hike, or building a stone wall, it can reengage the senses. It can reconnect isolated patches, islands of dulling senses and diminishing imagination, diminishing possibilities.

The other day, I was in my cabin working on fiction through a long green summer morning. Earlier a lion had caught a fawn, and the fawn's bleats had shaken me, as had, when I got up and went out to investigate, the sight of the lion leaping up from its hiding spot in the willows and running away. After that, it was a slow day for me, one in which I had trouble focusing. I've been using mostly analogies of lateral movement in discussing the travels on which fiction takes you, as if it were some horizontal surface along which you moved when going from the physical to the imagined; but I think it can also be described as travel along a vertical path. It often feels as if you were descending from the rock world, the real world, into the imagined one; and on a good day as if you could slip down into that chute, that shaft, into the below-place, easy as pie, like some subaqueous diver weighted with lead ankle wraps, or like some scientist suited up in an iron bathysphere: a quick descent, a gentle bump on the bottom, and you're there, and you can begin writing. Other days, though, it is as if you were full of air and could not sink beneath the surface — and certainly, on that day I heard the squawling and got up from my desk and walked out and flushed the lion up from out of those willows, the day turned raggedly (though wonderfully) into one of those days on which there can be no escape from the deep physical, no journeying across that gap into the deeply imagined. It was perhaps like being caught in a leghold trap.

I kept trying — working on a sentence, scratching it out. Trying it from another angle, scratching it out.

It was like a joke. My cabin's right at the edge of a vivid green marsh, full of life and rot. A south summer wind was blowing hard, sweeping laterally across the marsh, flattening the tall grass and slamming mountain-scent in through the open screened windows as I tried to descend, still juiced from the lion and juiced, too, now, from this, the incredible gusting wind, and the scents it brought, and all that green, green waving light. A wall of thundercloud came moving up the valley, rising like some wave larger than anything seen at sea, and it rolled in over the marsh and brought hail and then slashing rain, a drumming, shouting sound against my tin roof, deepening, in all that moisture, the smells of the marsh, crushing flowers, releasing the scent of wild strawberries after the sun came back out; and I had to just sit there, pen in hand, and float on the surface, unable even to get my head beneath the water.

Is there a story — are there stories — so important to tell that you could descend beneath this fury, such a day's *tempest*, find them, and deliver them to the reader? *Yes*; I believe there are.

Are such stories as real as the storm-lash itself — those precious few stories? *Yes*. Or *maybe*. *Yes*.

And then the kicker is this: in passing from the real to the imagined, in following that trail, you learn that both sides have a little of the other in each, that there are elements of the imagined inside your experience of the "real" world — rock, bone, wood, ice — and elements of the real — not the metaphorical, but the actual thing itself — inside stories and tales and dreams. You write a sentence about a hawk's swooping on a swallow and have no sooner finished it and looked up than you see feathers falling from the sky.

But still, for the most part, each resides in its own country: the real and the imagined; the actual and the possible. And it's important to keep the path, the trail, between the two open; important to keep the brush at least somewhat beaten back, to allow relative ease of passage between the two. Which brings us finally to the notion of why the daily doing of it is important — the writing of fiction, if that's what you do, and to a lesser extent, the reading of it. You've got to keep the grass worn down between the two worlds, or you'll get lost as shit; and sometimes you get a little disoriented, even with daily passages and explorations of the two further territories. You can't help but remember what Faulkner is alleged to have said when asked whether he wrote daily or only when the inspiration hit him. It's said he replied that he wrote only when the inspiration came, but that he made sure it came every morning at ten o'clock sharp when he sat down at his desk.

Another of these kinds of smart sayings I remember is one in which some prolific writer was asked how he'd managed to publish so many books. He said that it was quite easy: a page a day equaled a book a year. I've been working on my first novel for over twelve years now, and such statements give me encouragement and remind me that it's not just books that are important but also the sentences within them. It should be an obvious realization, but its implications become clear only when you do the math. The present draft of my novel is about 1,400 pages, which parses out to approximately one paragraph a day over those twelve years. The novel is, of course (I hope), nothing so boring as one paragraph from each day of my life over that twelve-year span, but rather a paragraph per day of a parallel and imagined life — which, after a dozen years of daily entering into and exiting from it, can make a writer increasingly a little goofy and also a bit tired, as if he or she were working one long stretch of double overtime, or had two families, or two lives.

We write fiction, I think, for very nearly the same reasons that we read it: to sharpen our senses and to regenerate those dead or dying places and parts within us where the imagination has been lost or is trying to be lost. Pine trees lose their needles every three years, and bears enter the earth, the dream-world, and float in sleep for five or six months at a time, but we humans are fragile and almost hairless, shivering on the earth, and our cells are dying and being reborn daily; we must eat often, and sleep nightly, pulled out each day by the sun. Almost all of our rhythms are compressed into parameters of one single earth's rotation. It is the rhythm into which we have evolved; it fits our bodies, physically, and it fits our minds and our imaginations. We can accumulate the days and their imaginings and then craft and create things beyond a day's work, but the days are our basic building blocks — a day's work is like a paragraph. To leave too many gaps in the thing being crafted or imagined, to work too erratically, is to run the risk, I'd think, of weakening with gaps and absences of rhythm the foundation and structure of the thing one is attempting to make real, or attempting to make be felt as deeply as if it *were* real.

That famous advice of Hemingway's is repeated often, about how a writer should leave a day's work slightly unfinished and at a point where he or she knows something of what will be in the next paragraph, to help facilitate the ease with which the rhythm may be resumed the next day. The descent of the bathysphere, vertically, or the morning trek into the woods, horizontally. The passage from here to there. The practice of staying supple rather than becoming brittle.

The daily doing of it is nothing less than a way to rage against constriction and entrapment, fragmentation and isolation, the poisonous seeds of our monstrous success in terms of our biomass and our effect upon the world, but at this cost: the erosion of the individual, the erosion of the specialist, the unique, the crafted.

The stories we tell in fiction — stories of warning or celebration, stories of illustrative possibility — are important. When the shit really hits the fan for a civilization, artists can become more important than ever, in helping to bend a culture back to another direction, away from the impending and onrushing brick wall.

I believe this. I believe that by crossing the path back and forth enough times, as if weaving something, fiction can become as real as iron or wood; that it can rust, rot, or burn; that it can nurture and nourish, or inflame. I believe that it can decide actions and shape movements, sculpt us more securely or intelligently (as well as more passionately) into the world, just as the continents on whose backs we are riding sculpt our cities, towns, and cultures.

I believe fiction can heal things, and I think we would all agree, now more than ever, that we can use some healing, and that we need it daily.

Phobia and Composition

RICK MOODY AND
MARGARET F. M. DAVIS

1

MY ACCOUNT: I always hated swimming lessons. This was on Weed Beach (in Darien, Connecticut), on the Long Island Sound. In recollection, Weed Beach feels oily, overcrowded, hemmed in symbolically by its proximity to New York Harbor and by the crowds from Rowayton and Darien who sought refuge there. I took after Mom's dad,

2

MY MOM'S ACCOUNT: Thirty-five years after the fact, that period of your language acquisition is recalled as a swirl of housepainting, house sale, being pregnant with your younger brother, your paternal grandparents moving from Boston to the area, your father quite ill with mononucleosis. Trying to be a "good" wife and mother to three children at age

F. M. Flynn — publisher of the New York Daily News — in some ways: left-handedness, redheadedness, tendency to sunburn. Thus, at the beach, I was always lacquered with various solvents to keep me from burning, and I was always burning anyhow. And then peeling. My brother nicknamed me Glue Factory.

But the worst part of the beach was swimming lessons. My sister and brother, on either side of me, were gifted swimmers, would spend hours in the flat calm of the South splashing and paddling. Not so with me. During my penultimate lesson (as I reconstruct it), with some teenage guy on holiday from a boarding-school or Ivy League swim team, it was decided that it was past time for me *to learn to float*. However, I was smart enough to know that rocks sank, that naval vessels plunged to the inky bottom of the seven seas, that only necromancy or supernatural powers would en-

twenty-six, a good sister, a good daughter (and daughter-in-law), was pretty exhausting.

No comes to mind as a possible first word: when you were about nineteen months and I was boiling everyone's underwear every day (Dwight had contracted a staph infection, so we all had to lather up with special soap EVERY day and go to elaborate lengths to prevent further infection . . . all this, and only one bathroom in the house), the enforcement of strict routine was stressful for us all. During this time, you developed the first of many bouts of strep throat, and around 2:00 A.M. you had a 104.5-degree fever. The doctor told me to give you alcohol sponge baths, since you would throw up the liquid aspirin. Never have I felt so much like a torturer, while you cried and cried and quivered, saying, "No more, no more!"

It was soon apparent that books were tremendously appealing to you, and I would put

able a person to traverse the surface. Furthermore, the basic human trust required for this (or other aquatic operations) was, as I saw it, unwise.

Nonetheless, the blond instructor persuaded me to lie out straight in his arms, as though I were an offering to Poseidon, and then, according to his secret knowledge, he began to remove his large hands, inch by inch, claiming that *if I held in a deep breath*, I would float upon the lazy swells. I would bob.

This was ludicrous. This was entirely contraindicated by *my personal investigations of the physics of suburban environments, the physics of tennis balls and leaf piles and rock-skipping and aggressive retrievers*, and so forth, and I began to scream and to clutch at the guy like some *Titanic* rescuee, though the water would barely lap at my waist. I fled back to my towel and would swim for no man or woman for a good five years thereafter.

Meredith on one side of me and you on the other and read most often from a big anthology of nursery rhymes and stories (I can show you the book). She would become bored after about fifteen minutes, but you would sit and listen as long as I had time to continue.

Somewhere around nursery-school age you liked to pretend that you were a different boy with another name (I can't remember the name). During this early period (and for some years to come), you deferred to Meredith on most things. I was thankful when she was in school all day, since it gave you some space from her always being "in charge."

Since we lived so close to Long Island Sound, we were around the water a lot in the summer. As you got older, you played at the edge but had no interest in getting your face in the water or learning strokes. You were pretty thin and got blue fast . . . who would find that fun? But later, when boats

In the single digits, I was sick a lot. I don't remember much about it, except the feeling of having two ear infections at once (this you don't easily forget), and, later, an Easter weekend in bed, after a tonsillectomy.

In general, I wasn't good with strangers. I avoided social events. My parents devised exercises for me, to improve my mettle. E.g., my mother sent me into a dry cleaner's in town to pick up my dad's shirts. The symbolism here is rich: *entrusted with the uniform of Dad's capitalist endeavor.* Moreover, I always really loved the smell of dry-cleaning chemicals. As well as the naphthalene of my grandmother's enormous closets (she had already confined herself to her bedroom by the time I was old enough to know her), in the pristine corridors where her things were stored in the house she shared with my grandfather.

Anyway, I went into the dry were the activity, your dad and I agreed that your learning to swim was absolutely vital. I sensed that you wanted to learn, but fear overtook you; after your uncle Jack died, we all went to Fort Lauderdale with my father for a ten-day February vacation . . . you were four and a half; you may remember flying on the private jet. I think your dad was mortified by how terrified you were of the water. Even your grandfather couldn't coax you into the pool for more than a few minutes.

When you were about five and we moved to Ironwood Lane, we met some people nearby whose daughter was giving swimming lessons. We signed both you and Dwight up for lessons twice a week. It was a generally chilly summer, with many rainy days. The lessons weren't really consistent (and in truth I think the teenager probably wasn't a very good teacher). Dwight made steady progress, but the girl told us

cleaner's, and it was forested with shrink-wrapped garments in a way I've always found inspiring, and I was feeling somewhat hopeful, until I saw *the dry cleaner himself* — an older man, in the predictably starchy professional uniform of the early sixties — thronged with brusque and affluent women looking for restitution in the matter of spots or stains or shrinkages.

I was paralyzed. Unable to proceed with my important mission. I suppose the specific problem had to do with *making my needs clear to this benevolent dry cleaner,* viz., making sure that my father's shirts were starched, proffering the ten, accepting the change. But surrounded by so many clamoring housewives, this was impossible for me. I slunk back outside to the car, made a weak excuse, and was reprimanded by my mother and induced to return tearfully to the store, with her, to stand patiently while the process of ex-

she was stumped as to how to get you over your sense of panic when you were asked to float along without a board. You complained when we talked about it, in that way that kids will, looking off into the distance and shuffling their feet. . . .

It was sad, but as far as your dad was concerned, you weren't allowed to quit until a day when he and I came to watch a lesson. You went into the water, made some tentative attempts to follow instructions, and then really got hysterical. I think I pulled you out, wrapped you in a towel, and we cut the whole lesson short, your dad then saying you wouldn't be coming back. I have a memory of him in a black mood in the car, driving home, saying, "What a waste of money!"

You also seemed to catch any germ that was floating about, and gradually it seemed that your tonsils and adenoids were the main target, becom-

change (legal tender for shirts, folded, in brown wrapping paper) took place, amid virtuosic pleasantries of the sort that I would never master. *See how easy it is?*

(This phobia reappeared in my twenties, when, in Hoboken, the only dry cleaner near me was given to a repartee overstuffed with flatteries. I'd beg my girlfriend to go in there for me, was utterly intractable about it, and in this way fell again into one of my many novel anxieties: *fear of dry cleaners.*)

Meanwhile, I was devouring the F. W. Dixon oeuvre. *The Hardy Boys and the Sunken Treasure,* etc. I also liked Encyclopedia Brown, who, like his coevals the Hardys, spent his pubescence solving neighborhood mysteries. I could never actually identify the criminals in these thrillers myself, and I didn't particularly give a shit who was responsible anyhow, but I admired the inventiveness of the crimes. I wanted to

ing chronically enlarged and swollen.

By the end of that kindergarten year, you had missed just about half the school days, and the doctor scheduled you twice for your tonsillectomy in the spring, but every time the date approached you'd get another cold and the date would have to be postponed. (I should interject here that it was in March of this year that my mother died, just eighteen months after Uncle Jack. She'd been hospitalized for about two weeks, and I'd been driving down to Westchester every other day.) Finally, the doctor said the only way to break this cycle was to hospitalize you for three to four days, load you up with medication, and do the surgery on the fifth day.

You couldn't seem to understand why all this was necessary, and you were very nervous about going. The first day went pretty well, but you got very annoyed at having to stay in bed. The nurses wouldn't allow you

be Encyclopedia Brown, of course, but I was actually getting pretty lousy grades in school. I got an X on Miss Rydell's history test in fourth grade, an original, new, *lowest possible grade* (she made clear to me), far lower even than the usual D. Mostly, my scholastic ambition was to avoid the anger of my teachers, and thereby the anger of my parents. Miss Rydell, however, was from Texas and had a thermonuclear temper (which she had visited upon my sister before me).

I loved television. I would watch reruns of old comedies all day long, and was also especially attracted to anemic science-fiction programming like *Lost in Space* and *Star Trek*. I was busy watching television, in fact, while my parents divorced. I remember nothing about their parting — beyond a particularly forlorn closed door in the living room one night, or a harsh exchange

to walk around. You'd ask about when you were leaving, and I'd tell you that you'd be coming home right after the operation. I recall being agitated at not being permitted to walk you down to the surgery. . . .

You were in awful pain when we brought you home. Our job was to do just about anything to keep you from crying a lot, because this would just irritate your throat more, making the pain worse. During that summer we bought the Ironwood Lane house and we were really preoccupied with that transition, which I believed would solve everyone's problems (that's how stupidly naive I was, at age thirty).

Physically, you improved remarkably. You certainly seemed happier. You were very successful at school and had some good friends. I still sensed that you were fearful of the rough-and-tumble that most of your peers (and your

on my father's sailboat —
and I guess that's because it
was essentially redundant (to
my knowledge, my parents
never once embraced in front
of me). Furthermore, I was
oblivious to the division of
their property, and the Mexi-
can legal proceedings, because
I was preoccupied with much
more traumatic news con-
cealed within this calamity:
We were going to move.

This was heartrending not
only because I was sick at the
idea of walking into a classroom full of strangers, but also
because I had recently begun
going steady with Susan Ward.
In proof thereof, I had kissed
the sleeve of her denim jacket,
its smudged and musty arm
registering indelibly upon the
scroll of my lifelong infatua-
tions. We played four-square
together. We spoke awkwardly
and hastily in the shadows of
oaks. Eventually, like a con-
sumptive nineteenth-century
lover, I told her of *my immi-*

brother) readily enjoyed. There
was a subtle but perceptible
undercurrent of anxiety. There
were nightmares and sleep-
walking (in that scary way
where you couldn't seem to
hear us talking to you but you
managed to walk downstairs).
When we carefully woke you,
you were terrified and disoriented.

As you learned to read, you
also learned to write with
frightening ease and lucidity.
We considered you extremely
bright and destined for great
things, as long as your "stamina" held up. Simmering in
the back of my mind was
Gramma's story of her brother
Albion, who had been overseas
in World War I, and when he
came back was constantly ill
and kept to his room for the
rest of his brief life. In short, I
was concerned that a certain
hypersensitivity (and propensity
to cry easily) would handicap
you.

Your father and I knew that

nent departure from Darien for-ever, believing that this would immortalize our bond. It didn't register much. However, I was happy to find in my limitless grief that James Taylor had written his morose "Fire and Rain" about her: *Suzanne, the plants they may put an end to you.* I didn't know what this botanical and eschatological riddle meant, of course, and the name of James's beloved was only an approximation of the name of my angelic Susan Ward, yet I believed, based upon this evidence, that my loss, my dislocation, *was as big as the Billboard Top Forty.*

I started at a new school. And then, a year after, I started at another. And we moved. And we moved again. And we moved yet again. And again. By the end of this hot streak of suburban addresses, wherein the Allied Van lines and their x-large corrugated cartons became routine, I became so disoriented that I planned my associations around the in-

you three would pick up on signals of trouble between the two of us, so by some unwritten agreement we simply didn't talk much, except late at night in red-faced whispers. We learned each other's "hot" buttons and also learned when to use this ammunition to best effect. We all know what happens when people suffer this too long: they become numb. What we did was go out A LOT. And drink A LOT. Your dad spent many evenings in New York City. Since he was mildly depressed most of the time, I became so as well.

I'm sure you all intuited the tension, though Meredith and Dwight say they never suspected any problems (I can't remember when or how the subject came up in the last five years, but it did). Here's my oblique prose, trying not to say that I think I was more psychologically preoccupied with myself than with monitoring the impact of a gathering storm. There was no trust between

evitability of leaving. In eighth grade, at the infernal Saxe Junior High School of New Canaan, local citadel of social repression and conformism, I actually kept a calendar *on which I counted off the days until we would pack up anew.* I started counting in the hundreds, crossing off the days, all the way down to zero.

I gave up trying to talk to people. I gave up trying, in speech, to address the spot where my childhood melancholy — whether it was situational or congenital — had formed itself into a little keloid bauble. I suppose this indicates a predestined selection in the choice between spoken word and silent scrawl, between *parole et langue.* I had phobias. I had conversation fear. I thought of conversations as the places where people stuck in their penknives. I trusted few. I kept my mouth shut. And I practiced writing. Writing was about improbably languid and slothful tempos, about relax-

your dad and me, on any level. How can I assess what impact that had on you three? At this point there weren't any obvious indicators of your adult difficulties . . . as best I can see.

Changing schools: this whole period after the divorce was really chaotic for me, too. I tried and tried and tried to find a way to get your dad to move out, so that your lives wouldn't be so additionally disrupted, but since he thought I really had "lost my mind," right up to the day we signed the papers I'm sure he thought I would relent and remain with him. His constant refrain was, "You're going to ruin the children. . . . This is all a totally selfish move on your part. I never have, never will want, a divorce. Go ahead, have an affair, just don't break the partnership." Even now, not many days go by that I am free of this guilt. How to put a good face on it? When I felt like the spaceman, Keir Dullea, sailing through the

ation and torpor, about meditative silence, about stillness, about music — like the music of my mom, in our mostly empty house on Valley Road in New Canaan, plunging into the sad opening movement of the "Moonlight Sonata" on an old upright.

One of the last things my family did together was go to see 2001: *A Space Odyssey*. Must have been at the Darien Playhouse (what did they think of it there?). The film was so beyond me, at eight years old, so disturbing, so baroque in its exposure of complex ideas, that it single-handedly created in me the ambition to use my imagination: HAL's struggle against the astronauts, those guys in the Cro-Magnon culottes juggling animal femurs, the Pan Am moon shuttle. I pestered my parents with questions on the way home: *If there's an edge to the universe, what's beyond the edge? If there was a moment*

black void in a tiny, soundless capsule?

You did have trouble making new friends after that time, but it didn't appear to bother Dwight in the least. . . . His troubles were delayed. At this point, I also realized I'd better get some additional income, and that meant I wasn't around as much. Still, you continued to perform in school in an above-average fashion. I'll mail you all the relevant report cards. I don't remember any major blowups, beyond your forgetting to let me know where you were going and when you'd be home (in those days, one could allow ten- and twelve-year-olds to bike around a two-mile radius without worrying that they might be kidnaped or molested). Of course, there was a lot of back-and-forth between my house and your dad's.

With your writing, our aim was to expand vocabulary and fluency by encouraging as much reading as you would

in which the universe was created, what was before that moment? Other kids in Fairfield County had the Presbyterian Church, or the Church of the Pop Warner Football League, but I was baptized in the murky font of the imagination, and I'm grateful for it. Once I was through with my Ur-texts, with Kubrick's film, with *The Odyssey*, with *Alice's Adventures through the Looking Glass*, I was never going to law school. And thus Banana Flair first smudges ruled notebook paper, in 10/71, or thereabouts, in this genuine excerpt from my juvenilia: "I *really* wonder about dinosaurs. I know about millions of kinds. Ones that are 50 ft. high. I wonder if I'm the biggest machine in the world, a curiosity machine, one big hunk of it" (italics in original).

Afraid of strangers, afraid of telephones, afraid of strangers on telephones, un-happily tolerate. You were in a family where this was as natural as breathing. Books were positively revered by my parents, too. When I was about three or four years old, a major house renovation took place, and during that work, large bookcases were added everywhere — in the old living room, in my room, and in Jack's new room. People read all the time. Someone was always reading TO me or reading WITH me. It seems to have been my major occupation, as I look back on the years before age nine or ten. No matter what excessive pile of Christmas or birthday presents came my way, books were always included. But I don't remember being able to talk about my reactions with anyone in the family, and perhaps just barely, superficially, with my best pals.

Anyway, the stage was set. Your father and I concentrated more on Meredith's reading because she was having so much trouble with concentration and

comfortable on airplanes, in crowds, afraid of public speaking, afraid of open spaces, of confinement, of women, daylight, heights, *people*, and so on. Afraid.

I came to write, therefore, because I was too timid to be a raconteur, because the giddy freedom of imagination (as it is rendered in language) was best and most comfortably practiced, for me, alone, away from the tempests of schoolyard bluster. I wondered why I was made this way, sure, when the contrary seemed the norm for other people, and it was on this question that I first concentrated my energies, as writing often compels itself toward *unspeakable* (Donald Barthelme's word) interrogatives, things that can't, inside the Foul Pole of everyday life, really be *said*, or are ignored because of the kind of responsibilities they entail, as those words *I Love You* are pretty hard to say (I don't say them

focus. But you would very quietly pick up many of the books she had and polish them off. In your case, I'm reminded of an article on the pianist Yvgeny Kissin, who was described as only becoming really animated and dynamic when he was playing, having spontaneously learned music before he could talk. I think you learned that exquisite pleasure of abandoning oneself to a fictitious world at a very early age. . . .

By the time you were perhaps eight or nine years old, you spoke of wanting to be a writer. . . . Since I couldn't get my own act together in this area, I was determined to do what I could, at an early stage of your growth, to motivate and supply what "tools" I could discover that might help you see this as a definite path.

I think I've about exhausted what memory I have on this topic. I feel awkward and embarrassed about trying to describe your shyness . . . strange!

enough to the writer in the next column over, for example), until eventually the process of considering these questions is itself enough, as distinct from the entrapment of answers — leaving behind, in the sheer music of questions, in medias res, as Montaigne says, "some idea of my habits and opinions."

Which is not to say that I don't see you as being reclusive and depressive: I just don't understand where "shy" fits in. Are shy people phobic? Was it the alcoholism and its concomitant handicaps that make you shy? You ask how I recognize you, then . . . as a beloved son, in whom resides a lot of my own sad history.

Secret Agent

DENIS JOHNSON

I'M REMEMBERING A TIME in Chicago. Down around Jefferson Street, some ways below the Loop. I couldn't even guess how far below now, twenty-one, -two, -three years later. This was the very bad wino district around 4:00 A.M. People without soul or spirit slept against walls or right in the gutter, as they'd been warned they might someday if they kept on . . . and they'd kept on. This dark morning I'd come here to find work in the day-labor gangs the state employment people formed on weekdays, but I sensed I'd be living here, too, someday, and I observed electrically and sadly my future all around me, people with dull faces nodding like toys and fingering the tatters of their clothes and exploring their lips with their tongues. Soon one place opened for business in the neighborhood, a giant tavern with big windows and no name — just a white marquee running the whole length of the building, reading SHOT AND A BEER 25¢. I recall it now, this place, as an island of horrific light. It was illuminated inside with fluorescent ceiling lamps and jammed with people who moved around as if they were all on fire. I didn't go in. A bum woke up in the gutter right beside where I stood looking from across the street. He felt in the waist of his pants and came up with a pint bottle, half full. He tipped it up, and it gurgled steadily until he'd emptied it all down into him. I was only twenty-four or -five, but already I could have told you how important it tasted. And the people who kissed the feet of Christ could have told you how it tasted. I saw everything there in the gutter — the terror and the promise. Later I spent the morning in the smoky Day Labor Division with better than a hundred men who'd learned how not to move, learned how to stay beautifully still and let their lives hurt them, white men with gray faces and black men with yellow eyes. I worked the rest of the week in a factory without ever comprehending exactly what was manufactured there, and at night I'd get drunk and shut myself in a phone booth and call the woman in Minnesota who'd broken my heart. The calls were full of laughter and dreams because I was happy to be working and even happier to be drunk. Eventually she relented, said she'd join me in Chicago, in the streets, by the lake, in the parks — it seemed as if this city had been built and had waited its whole history for somebody feeling as good as me to step into it and make it live. What was I going to do with all of this? Where could I make my monument to these simple triumphs and these complicated sorrows?

I heard on the BBC today a news report from a torn-up African nation, and I recognized the reporter's voice — I met her down there some years back. As I listened to her describe the deteriorating situation in those eerie surroundings, I remembered how much she enjoyed being in the thick of things. It occurred to me that I know what it's like at the hotel she's staying in, because I've stayed there, too. I'm acquainted with her favorite cab driver, the one she uses all the time in that town, and I've been to the U.S. Embassy there, which she describes now as pocked with bullet holes. I've seen many U.S. embassies pocked by bullet holes, and in fact I cowered behind the embassy in the country just east of the one she's now reporting from one afternoon while it was attacked by rebels, and I heard their bullets whizzing by as they tried to pock my head with holes. Thinking about all this, it occurs to me how many of my most boyish boyhood dreams have come true.

I wanted to be a Spy, a Secret Agent. To get in undetected, to deal with inscrutable forces in exotic worlds, and get out unscathed. Then I became too old to allow myself to want that anymore. I required myself to tell people I wanted something less fantastic. I told them I wanted to be a writer.

And eventually I became a free-lance writer traveling to these unhappy places full of danger and chaos. The others, the real journalists, the regularly employed, they sneer at me. I'm a cheap adventurer. I'm taking up space among people who have to be there. But in my story they're a pack of lemmings who don't care about the truth or the feeling or the sights and sounds or the faces and the voices — only about the stock images, the stock phrases, the news that's making everybody tired.

I'm not here to get the news. I'm making a story. I get in any way I can, and I stand in a burning city, revolted and ecstatic, inhaling the dust of old murders, the stench of corpses, not just satisfying naive childhood yearnings for adventure but pursuing some deeper vision of howling chaos — engaging in the same pursuit, in fact, as these maniac boys destroying everything with their weapons. This is what I'm here to do — to be one character in the middle of it all, a person both exonerated and ashamed.

And all I have to do to gain entry to this world is claim that I'm a writer. And the only one I have to convince of that is myself.

As I came to accept my role as profoundly different from theirs, instantly the other journalists began to tolerate and even to welcome me. I'm here only to enjoy one of the great freedoms, that of having no choice but to trust the moment and everyone in it; I'm here to taste the giddy joy in understanding that any other moment is utterly inaccessible, and that this one belongs to these strangers who may help you or kill you, these Third World guerrillas or jungle denizens or this character in sunglasses who resembles Peter Lorre and claims to have powerful friends in the Junta. . . . I'm making a story. And I get to be in it.

I stopped in for breakfast at Jean's Home Plate Café this morning, a little reluctantly, because Jean had complained that she was going blind the last time I was in there, and a biopsy was scheduled, something about her left eye. I've always liked her, and she's always had scraps for my dog, Harold, and insisted on going out to my truck herself to feed him, but now, if she were truly ill, like very much so, like with fatal cancer, our friendship would deepen beyond her fondness for Harold and my admiration for her biscuits and gravy. So I went to the Home Plate this morning not only for breakfast, but also to pass through the doorway of a mild form of fear and greet her. But her son was cooking, not Jean. "Where's Jean?" I said. "She passed away last night," he said. It wasn't her left eye but her lungs that killed her. He told me about the details. The guy beside me pointed out the telephone and the electric fan he'd bought for Jean. I also had details, for instance, about how she fed my dog. I almost turned down the breakfast, but her boy was there to cook in her honor, and so in her honor I ate. We talked about elk hunting and about Fort Lewis outside of

Tacoma, Washington, and other things — you know how it is, all those universes going on while one blanks out. It seemed strange to suddenly remember my girlfriend two hours earlier with her little boy, wrapping a piece of tape backward around her hand to sop up the albino dog hairs off his black Dracula suit. It's Halloween. Yellow leaves lay all over the dark pavements as I drove home to write this. It's what I do. Jean's son is a cook. So he cooked today. The children will be children, the people will be people, all things even down to the smallest will be as they are this day after Jean's death.

The Lousy Rider

ELIZABETH GILBERT

1

WHEN I LIVED OUT WEST, I knew a cowboy named Hank.
I admired him a great deal. He was a drunk, and he was belliger-
ent, and when he spoke it was mostly through curses. He could
not really articulate himself otherwise. For instance, he called
every inanimate object "the bitch," as in "Give me the bitch," instead of "Please pass me the sugar." I once brought Hank a thermos of coffee while he was saddling his horse at dawn. He set the
thermos on the ground, where he kept accidentally tripping on it
and kicking it over.

"Fuck!" he finally shouted in frustration. "I'll just drink the
bitch!"

I liked Hank so much. I was in Wyoming because I wanted to
be a professional cowgirl and because I wanted to be a tough character. I wanted to be just as tough as Hank, so I hung around him
all the time, imitating him.

"Fuck!" I'd shout, at the slightest provocation. "Fuck! Bitch!"

Hank wasn't given to tender moments of reflection, but one afternoon we were riding our horses along a mountain pass and — quite out of nowhere — he said to me, "You're a really good rider, you know."

I was so pleased. I blushed, in fact, because it was the best compliment I had ever received, and from the most unlikely source.

"Are you serious, Hank? You really think so?"

"I wish I was as good a rider as you," he said. "You're just a natural."

Now, Hank was one of those people who rode before they walked, so this was really saying something. This was actually the best moment of my life.

"That means so much to me, Hank," I said.

Hank was quiet for a long time, and then he said, "It's true. I wish I could express myself the way you do."

There was a long beat.

Then I asked, "Sorry, did you say that I was a good rider? Or did you say that I was a good *writer*?"

Hank laughed. "I said *writer!*" he shouted. "Fuck! I said you were a good goddamn *writer!*"

I was devastated by this misunderstanding — I already knew I could write; I wanted to *ride* — but to Hank it was a major laugh riot. "You really thought I wanted to ride like you? You really thought *I* would call *you* a natural rider? Ha!"

"Ha," I said, weakly.

"You're a lousy rider," he said. "But you're a goddamn good writer."

Not immediately thereafter, but very soon thereafter, I gave up on being a tough cowgirl and moved back East, where I began writing again. We are, after all, what we are. And sometimes, when we are trying to find a calling, it is helpful to confirm that we are not really very good at anything else.

2

My husband — who is not a writer — dreamed one night that he was one. In this dream he was a journalist on assignment, and his job was to cover a massive convention of police officers. The convention was held in a major arena, and when my husband the "journalist" stepped inside, he saw uniformed cops everywhere. He took out his notebook and tried to think of a good lead for his article. He thought and he thought. And then he wrote this sentence: "I walked into a sea of blue."

In his dream, my husband knew this was a lousy, cornball lead, but he couldn't think of anything better. He stared and stared at the cops, but this was the very best he could come up with. *I walked into a sea of blue.* He gazed at his notebook, depressed. Still asleep, my husband had a big revelation.

Gosh, he thought. I could never be a writer.

Now, I kept a diary as a child. I started it in second grade, and I kept it up with pretty good discipline. For the most part, my diary was a dry chronicle of my schedule ("Today I went to piano lessons. Yesterday I went to gymnastics"), but sometimes an event would occur that was actually worth *writing* about, and then I would rise to the occasion. One winter's day, my parents took me sledding after an ice storm, and it was very exciting and it really got my seven-year-old pulse racing, so I wrote about it in my diary. I described my sledding adventure this way: "Let me tell you, it was like riding a Thoroughbred that just got stung by a bee."

I remember writing that sentence. I remember sitting back and reading it over, gazing at my diary. I remember my revelation, too, which went something like this: Hey, that's not bad at all.

3

There are some excellent writers in my family, and everyone is a good storyteller. My great-grandfather was the best. He once wrote a letter to my uncle beginning, "I have just received a missive from that well-known illiterate your father, whose only use of the mother tongue is to order more hay for the pathetic assemblage of quadrupeds he insists on calling horses."

He could really turn a phrase, and so could his children. His only daughter was my grandmother, who was a famous wit (she once told me that Poughkeepsie was the Indian name for "Place Where Vassar College Is," and said of an irritatingly upbeat neighbor, "Every time that goddamn woman sees me in the grocery store, she has an orgasm"). My father was her favorite child, and she indulged him to an extreme because he was such a wisecracker. When he got married, my grandmother told my mom, "I should have laughed at him less and beat him more. I'm terribly sorry, Carol, but he's all yours now."

Then I was born, and I soon started telling stories, too. When I was in fourth grade, I came home from my first day of school and did such a riotous imitation of my flaky young hippie schoolteacher that my dad had to wipe tears of laughter from his eyes and blow his nose into his napkin. I grotesquely exaggerated every detail of this perfectly decent woman while my parents laughed and laughed, egging me on. It evidently never occurred to them that they should try to instill in me some respect for my elders. God bless them, they just thought I was entertaining.

Now they are proud of me because I am officially a writer. Despite all the good writers in my family, nobody else had ever done it officially, and this is all a pretty big deal. When I called my father at work to tell him that my first short story had been accepted for publication by a famous national magazine, he shut his office door and wept. He said, "I'm so proud of you! And to think that I knew you when you were just a babe in swaddling clothes!"

4

When my husband was a teenager, he wanted to be a magician. He studied magic on his own and learned how to do goofy tricks with handkerchiefs and doves. He performed for Girl Scouts and nursing-home inhabitants in his small Ohio town. He used to tell me stories about this, and I thought they were the funniest and saddest stories in the world. He showed me pictures of himself, all skinny and redheaded, brandishing his magic cane, and he was so earnest in the photographs that it would make me laugh and cry to see them. I think the laughing-crying stories are the best kind, so I became consumed with the notion of writing about a gawky teenage kid from Ohio who desperately wants to be a magician. I thought the whole topic was beautifully tragic.

I had been working on that story for a few months when I ran into an old friend, and she got to telling me a story herself. She told me about how her father's beloved cat had disappeared several months earlier. Apparently this event caused her father to lose his mind with grief, and he eventually became convinced that his nice neighbors had stolen his pet. He went utterly mad with delusion and paranoia. He stalked and threatened the nice neighbors for months and finally attacked the nice neighbors, and then had to be hauled away to a mental ward. In the end, though, someone discovered that the nice neighbors really *had* had the man's cat the whole time. They actually had stolen it. Nobody knew why. Too late this information emerged, because my friend's father's life had already been ruined.

An interesting story. A true story. And some freakish neuron in my system told me to combine it with my story of the gawky teenage magician. The freakish neuron had a sweet, reassuring voice that said, "Trust me, just do it." But by this point, the gawky-teenage-magician story had taken some strange twists of its own. The gawky teenager had became a brilliant middle-aged Hungarian immigrant who — though not a magician himself — owned a magic club and was obsessed with the lost arts of skilled European conjurers. Also, he was a murderer and an ex-con. He lived in a big house with his daughter, who was a talent-free aspiring magician, and with his brother-in-law, who was North America's greatest living sleight-of-hand artist. What had happened to the skinny kid from Ohio? I do not know, but he was nowhere to be seen.

So I gave the Hungarian immigrant a cat, had the cat disappear, and had the Hungarian become convinced that the nice neighbors had stolen the cat. The Hungarian went mad, and stalked and threatened the nice neighbors, and had to be hauled off to a mental ward. And the nice neighbors really *did* have the cat the whole time. Surprise! And I worked day and night on that story, but it just wouldn't come together. The stolen cat made no sense. The story made no sense. Why would a murderous Hungarian magic enthusiast lose his mind over a cat? Why would anyone? I wished I had never listened to the freakish neuron in the first place.

And then one day I was sitting in the New York Public Library, struggling with my work, when it struck me. I sat up in my seat and exclaimed loudly, "It's not a cat! It's a rabbit!" Of course it was a rabbit! It had to be a rabbit! What animal would be most treasured by a family of magicians? What is the traditional pet of magic? Not a stupid cat, but a rabbit. A rabbit! A rabbit! A rabbit!

I really wrote that bitch then.

The action all fell into place, into perfect order, and it was sad and funny, just as I had hoped it would be, back when it was still a story about a gawky teenage magician from Ohio, but it was *better* this way. The lost rabbit was a beautiful tragedy; the Hungarian's madness was heartbreaking; the neighbor's betrayal sickened the conscience. To me, the ending felt so correct and so appropriate that it seemed to bend over backward to kiss the beginning. How excited was I? I was so excited that I almost started barking in the New York Public Library. I almost started chasing my own tail because — let me tell you — it really *was* like riding a Thoroughbred that had just gotten stung by a bee. To write like that? Even for one hour? It really *was* like pulling a rabbit out of a hat. It really *was* like walking into a sea of blue.

Writing

WILLIAM VOLLMANN

The way of thinking that you reproach is the sole
consolation of my life.

MARQUIS DE SADE,
prison letter to his wife

I WRITE THIS BY HAND, with swollen and aching fingers.
Sometimes the ache oozes up to my shoulders, sometimes only to
my wrists; once or twice I've felt it in my back. Poor posture, they
say, or "repetitive stress injury," or possibly carpal tunnel syn-
drome; when for a price of five hundred or a thousand dollars they
administered electric shocks to my hands and arms to determine
the relative health of my nerve sheaths (the current made my
limbs jerk, in obedience to the highest laws of galvanics, and a
premedical spectator laughed), I was told that my case was either
moderate or severe. Subject to respites occasioned by voyages or
stints of block-printing, I have woken up with pain, and slept with
pain, my sweetly constant mistress, for seven years now, ever since

my thirtieth birthday. While there have been times when I could not close my hand around a water glass or turn the pages of a book, mostly this pain is an unobtrusive companion, a chronic irrelevance when I am loving my work, a chronic warning when I am not, in either case acknowledged and respected for having so steadfastly guested me, but rarely listened to: pain gives always the same advice, the wisdom of prudes and legislators, to stay within the limits. This pain of mine certainly does. Pain's advice is also that of my own heart, which used to tell me when I was in elementary school that if I could only escape the chalkboards and inky desks, running away into sunny fields of milkweed, I would find my destiny. If I weren't writing, who knows what brighter life I would find? My pain respects me, being in no wise related to the shouting tyrant endured by puking heroin addicts in withdrawal, burned children, soldiers gassed or shot in the stomach. When I think of them, I love my pain more for being so undemanding, for letting me do almost everything I want to do. Yes, I worry sometimes about future damage, having met old ranch hands whose hands were but blackened hay-baling hooks. Writing is bad for me physically, without a doubt, but what would I do if I stopped?

The nights of sleepless excitement are almost reduced to memories now. They possess me but once or twice a year. I no longer feel, as I did at seventeen or twenty, that I am an ecstatic vessel bubbling over with words — words gushing from my hands like sparks, forming at my will or beyond my will in armies upon paper and screen, the letterforms themselves beautiful, the combinations of words likewise beautiful to eye, ear, lips, and heart. Now I feel instead that the tale is a block of darkness that I chip away at deliberately until I begin to glimpse tiny stars within; I seek to unveil as many of these as I can, leaving just the right amount of darkness behind them to make them shine the brighter by contrast, protecting them from the day. I labor where before I played. In part this change is due to the pain in my hands. But another reason is that what once came easily would now come *too* easily. The thrill of writing, as of pure animal sexuality, derives from newness. Following newness faithfully must bring us farther and farther out of school, until the milkweeds loom around us. The difficult way is the way that I want to go. I write less and less for "success," though for financial reasons I will always try to write for publication. I write to discover the universe and to discover myself. My writing is thus, for me, a deeply selfish act. Very often, what I discover infects me with sadness, even with anguish. This voyage that I am taking into the block of darkness leaves me night by night more alone.

Example: I am on the verge of concluding a long essay on violence that it has taken me sixteen years to write. My three American commercial publishers have all turned it down, mostly unread. I am sad about this to the extent that the middling advance (thirty thousand dollars, say, spread over two or three years, if I was lucky) and the minor increase in "recognition" that publication might have brought me would have benefitted my career — that is, enabled me to continue writing in comfort. That is why I will try some academic presses now. I am also sad because I love books as objects, and it would be a pleasure for me to hold my finished work in my hands. I am otherwise indifferent. I am fortunate enough to make money writing elsewhere. If the manuscript remains unpublished in my lifetime, I will entomb it somewhere, out of respect for what I learned in the writing, but without much regret. For the secret (which actually is no secret, since you who read this either know it in some sense already or will never know it) is this: Writing is an intense joy, as faithful as pain, as beautiful as love; making beauty is love, is making love; and that is what writing is.

Every joy that I have ever experienced, even the most physiological, ultimately reaches me as aesthetic. Whether writing is knowing or whether it is singing, the love remains, the joy, the daring, the exaltedness when one approaches, at however far a remove, perfection. Shake the greatest art ever, and dross will come out. But honest effort for its own sake is beauty. If the writer is talented and lucky enough, then the result may be beautiful, too. (I use the word *lucky* advisedly. We credit Petrarch's genius alone for his sonnets. But what if he had never met his Laura? Can we credit him for her existence, or for the effect that she had on him?) If the result is beautiful, then others can see it and feel it. But look through a camera at a face or a landscape, and you may see the perfection of it even if you fail to trip the shutter, or if you set the wrong f-stop. Write a bad poem, and you still may have seen God or gained enlightenment at the feet of the devil.

Sometimes I sit by the ocean in southeast Asia, or walk toward a subarctic horizon glittering with crowberries, and I think: This is enough. I am here; I have seen this; to the best of my capacity, I have known this. This is beautiful. And then I let it go. The perceiving is all the writing that I feel called upon to do. And other times I awake from a terrifying or dazzling dream, and I know that if I don't write it down now, its filmy coherence will rupture into a million shrinking droplets, like certain kinds of ink trying to dry upon acrylic. After all, so what if I forget that dream? How many faces, flowers, and rivers have I forgotten? Maybe they've sunk into me, and I draw from them without knowing it, or maybe I simply have the sense that I could only mar any conception I have of them by trying to translate it into groups of letters. But the dream calls to me, cries out for me to save it. Or a story comes into my head. Or the voice of someone who loves me speaks to me. Or an idea, an inhuman crystal, attacks me with its colors, just as strange ores and fossils attack the rockhound, their possibilities overruling his tranquillity so that he must take up his hammer and get on his walking boots.

How can I possibly have the effrontery to believe that any of this will be significant to you? When I go into a museum I see the clusters of tender, avid, or dutiful faces around the fad-pieces of the moment; and then at unpredictable intervals an unknown work will catch somebody's soul (or maybe his feet will get tired); and surrounding these hang the crucified legions of the unregarded. Which category will the books I write be placed in? How can I know, and how does it depend on me? Does what I write seem beautiful to me? That is all that I can know and count on, and it is enough. But if it seems beautiful to you, too, I am grateful. I like to please people. I like to be, as ticket collectors say, "validated." I like to make a living.

But I'm beginning to wonder whether someday I ought to prove my love. De Sade proved his in prison. Homes without bookshelves, people who don't mind *le mot juste* but will settle for any old approximation, readers without enough time to finish a short story — these signs of the times, like the pain in my wrists, which at the moment nibbles at my palms, all remind me that my days are numbered. How long will this world continue to support my easy life? I believe in my sincerity; I believe that I am willing to suffer for the sake of the word; but the pain in my hands is only a promise, not a demonstration like de Sade's ranting and masturbating behind the prison door, refusing to renounce his terrifying lusts, or Hans and Sophie Scholl's going to the scaffold for writing anti-Nazi pamphlets, or Joan of Arc's eloquently defying the inquisitors who will burn her. How can I prove myself? How can I love more? For now, the answer is to keep writing, whatever happens, to try to do better, to go where I must, listening to joy. De Sade, the Scholls, and Joan didn't choose to be afflicted, and I hope never to be tested as they were. I know that I love what I do. I hope that my life (for which I give thanks) glides on and on, and that like a good prostitute, I can continue to convert joy into cash.

For the Money

MARK JACOBSON

WHAT OTHER REASON could there be? For my soul? Gimme a break. Maybe Stephen King doesn't write for the money. Then again, he has a lot of money. So why shouldn't he write for the money?

I write for the money. Sure, there are other, subsidiary reasons. Sometimes writing gets my rocks off. My spiritual rocks, my data rocks, my attention-to-craft rocks, my pet rocks. Sometimes a writer can be like a blues musician: you be playing that same riff over and over again and sometimes truth jus' seep out. After all, modes of human expression being highly circumscribed in their ability to convey various forms of information, it makes sense that certain truths can be revealed only by writing. This may be the true value of writers, since they write so much more than non-writers, therefore making them likelier to discover truths accessible only through typing. Indeed, if every writer has within himself that famous tribe of monkeys which, given enough time and paper, would come up with all the great works of the world, there's no limit to the Truth a writer might unearth in his lifetime. Writers are just chockfull of potential Truth.

Still, there is no more perfect answer to the why-we-write question, no more compelling reason to write, than: *for the money*.

Almost all of my favorite writers wrote for the money. Someone once asked Philip K. Dick, certainly one of the greatest novelists of the twentieth century, why he wrote, and he said, "The two thousand dollars," which is how much Dick got for most of his paperback sci-fi novels. Two thousand dollars for *The Three Stigmata of Palmer Eldrich*, two thousand dollars for *Time out of Joint*, two thousand dollars for *Martian Time-Slip*. Two thousand bucks for masterpieces! But then again, two thousand bucks bought a lot of amphetamines in those days, and since Dick liked to speed while writing, that two thousand dollars probably enabled him to make another two thousand dollars and another two thousand dollars after that. So it was a good investment. Besides, how else was Philip K. Dick going to make two thousand dollars — being a plumber? *Martian Time-Slip* was probably the only book he could write at that particular time, and two thousand dollars was what they were paying. Take it or leave it, Philip K. Dick.

Me, I'm no Phil Dick, but I've got the same problem. How else am I going to make the two thousand dollars? I'm a writer, and if they're paying two thousand dollars, that's what they're paying.

Since I quit cabdriving, in 1974, I haven't made a penny doing anything else except writing. No other money comes in. Plus, I'm stubborn. The only work I'll do is write. I won't do anything else. No teaching. No little woodshop in Vermont where I lovingly refurbish antique guitars. I make a living by writing. This way, when people ask me what I do, I say write, and that's that.

There's some Oedipal angle here, now that I really go deep-dish on this why-I-write deal. I do it to dis Dad, not that he deserves it, much. The incident in question dates back to eleventh grade, when my parents paid for a course that might improve my SAT scores, which were shockingly low for someone of Jewish extraction. Part of the deal was a "college/career-counseling session" attended by my father and myself, during which I was to be advised which institution of higher learning would most maximize my meager prospects.

"What do you plan to do for a living?" the counselor asked.

"I thought I'd be a writer," I replied, unexaminedly.

It slithered out, a surprise even to myself. After all, I didn't seem the type. I wasn't one of those sickly, bookish Southern boys left home from the hunting trips and football games. I grew up in Flushing, Queens, and if I read at all, it was the Hardy Boys, DC Comics, *Mad* magazine, and the occasional Quentin Reynolds biography of some figure like General Custer. Words themselves had little seductive quality to me, except maybe the words of a stray high school girlfriend saying, "OK, I'll do it." Never one to wear long, flowing Irish knit scarves on the Q17 bus, I had no romantic attachment whatsoever to the writer's life, no burning need to tell anyone beyond my friends how I felt about anything.

The reason I told that phony career counselor that I'd make my living as a writer had mostly to do with a snide comment issued by my tenth-grade English teacher. He'd never liked me, preferring to dote on the smart girls with their perfectly tortured interpretations of *Catcher in the Rye*. Not that I'd done much to warrant his attention. I'd been messing up, not handing in assignments, failing tests. Then the class was assigned a theme entitled "Yesterday Afternoon." As it turned out, my previous day had been spent at the Polo Grounds, the ancient, decaying ballpark where, in 1962, the home-team New York Mets would lose 120 games. On that particular afternoon, Marvelous Marv Throneberry, a player of legendary incompetence, hit a triple. Or at least it seemed like a triple, in the sense that Marv was standing on third base. Too bad he missed second base. First, too. So I wrote about that, and the teacher, probably one of those proto-intellecto baseball snobs in the making, liked it.

"Finally," he said, "something you're good at."

Finally something I was good at . . . funny what you take to heart. From that moment on, I thought I'd be a writer.

Dad did not see it this way. "No one makes a living being a writer," he interrupted. "He'll be a teacher," my father, a teacher himself, said to the career counselor.

Poor old Dad, he was an artist, a beautiful carpenter. But he grew up in the Depression, son of immigrants, and he knew a Jew couldn't make a living carving pieces of wood. So he became a shop teacher and bored himself silly watching the same snotty teenager make the same crappy bookshelf for forty years. Maybe that's why I decided to make my money, such as it is, as a writer. Unshackled from an immigrant sense of limitation through the unstinting labor of my mother's and father's civil-servant careers, I wanted to show that their labors had not been in vain. That I was a real American, someone without a ceiling. Rather than defy my father's wishes, the very act of my making a living as a writer would avenge his hemmed-in life.

So what's it been like, writing for money? Well, it's got its ups and down. Ins and outs. When you've got only one employee in your little-ass company, when responsibility cannot be delegated, the hours can be long, the road rough. Especially for the midlist guy, which, up to now, is the kind of guy I've been. As a midlist guy, you come to understand the exact value of your writing.

The first piece of writing I ever sold was a magazine article about underground discotheques. It was 1973; I was driving a taxi at the time and kept taking gay men to run-down warehouses on the West Side of Manhattan. One night I got invited inside. Beyond the gray steel door was a fabulous party in a huge room, an updated speakeasy. Sure, I'd been up to the Apollo, but I'd never seen so many blacks and whites dancing together, for sure not these kind of blacks and whites. There was something about it that struck me as news. So I hung out a bit, wrote an article about the scene. A friend said I could sell the piece to the *Soho Weekly News*, an Ur-sort of downtown paper that paid ten dollars. But the editors hated what I wrote and sent me into the drizzle on Broome Street. Then another friend said to send it to *New York* magazine, which sounded impossibly straight, but worked. They bought the story and gave me a thousand dollars. It was the exact same piece, now one hundred times more valuable.

It's something that always blows my mind: the price. How much things are supposed to be worth. After all, writing is a business like any other, subject to prevailing market factors. Every word I write, every notion I have, however half-baked, is for sale. I'm trying to make a living here, you understand? I'm a little idea factory, so why shouldn't every minimeme sprung from my ever-fecund brainpan cost somebody something? To this end, I've cut down on my pot smoking. Smoking makes me talk, spritz, tell jokes and stories, offer unsolicited cultural critiques, make political judgments, extend narratives. I heedlessly spew these potential gold mines into the idle ozone. This is bad commerce, a shot in the foot of personal intellectual copyright. Out here in the info jungle, asset protection is paramount. Loose lips sink ships. In paranoia there is profit.

I wish I could stick to these highly reasonable credos, exercise a little self-discipline. Then I wouldn't have to write for the money. I'd be rich. I could write for the love of the language, things like that. Except I get rattled. Every time the boiler blows, or a child's mouth opens for orthodontia, or they tow away my car, I sweat. That's when I make the usual pronouncements about how I have to get organized, how I've got to act more like I'm running a small business, get Andrew Tobias's *Managing Your Midlist Money* on the computer. I go global then, sizing up the market so as to give my little economic engine every advantage in the current postmodernist landscape. For instance, I have diversified over the years, expanded into new forms. After twenty years as a journalist, I became a novelist, published a few of those books. I'd never even written (much less published) a short story before, but it's good to have more weapons in the old quiver, so to speak. Flexibility furthers. This creative switch-hitting is ideal for me, psychologically speaking. When I get sick of everyone, I write novels, and when I get sick of myself, I write journalism; it's a fifty-fifty thing, depending on whom I happen to hate more at the moment, me or them.

At this juncture it might be useful to include A Note on the Movies, seeing that any writer in this day and age who says he writes "for the money" cannot afford to ignore the sucking pull of Hollywood's massive cash machine. Duh, but do I have to mention that magazines don't pay that well (never more than fifteen thousand dollars for months of hard work)? As for novels, my standard line is: I was looking for a lower-paying profession than journalism, so I took up novel writing. But as a movie (re)writer, I once lucked into a situation where I made thirty-five thousand dollars a week (for three weeks) revamping one of the worst pictures ever shot. Numbers like this addle the mind. In fact, the price paid to movie writers has probably done more to alter the face of American narrative than any other factor. I mean, if you've got a story that might actually play as a movie, don't you owe it to yourself to try to make it a screenplay? And if that story isn't exactly suited to films (anyone with a modicum of cultural literacy can tell the difference between a tale told better as a novel, short story, movie, comic book, etc.), wouldn't you be tempted to crush it into the movie form anyway?

What are your choices for this perfect movie story? Write it as a novel, thereby spending two years on something that should take only three months? Or throw it away? The scrap heap of twentieth-century narrative is heavily laden with such tales misfiled into the wrong form. But what do you want *me* to do about it? I'm a midlist guy! I'm not taking responsibility for the demise of American storytelling. No way. I mean, fuck those Hollywood guys anyhow. Corporate jerk-offs, I don't care how much they're paying.

I just bring this up as a sample of the omnipresent difficulties facing the writer-for-hire. Reflexive antiauthoritarian personality traits can interfere with clear thinking. I may write for the money, but there's only a certain amount of money (not so much, alas) available to the sort of guy/writer I am. As a midlist guy, I accept the vagaries of my particular talents and tolerances.

I understand that plans go awry. My most recent plan: to turn out a 227-page (about) novel every year and half, build a little audience, make a living that way, until I die. Unfortunately, my most recent book, the great, criminally overlooked comic masterpiece *Everyone and No One*, published by Villard, seems to have come and gone without even having the chance to gather dust on the Barnes and Noble shelves. This is no reason to be discouraged, I tell myself. Audiences are not built in a day; amid the thick rain of books flying out of the publishing-industry thresher, things get lost. Even if the book just blew, well, that's fine: the plan was to keep on writing, not to care if they weren't all gems.

Still, when you write for the money, you've got to protect yourself. Weigh the long run and short run. So here I am, typing this little missive from my new cubicle at *New York* magazine, the semivenerable, midlist-accessible entity where my first work was published twenty-five years ago. It's cool. Journalism's got its various rhythms, and I've always been partial to weeklies. The short lead time cuts down the space for editorial meddling. Plus, they offered me a health plan. In the free-lance world you don't ask the second question when they offer you a health plan. Besides, it never hurts to get out of your room, learn a new thing or two while planning the next opus. Except that's the hassle, when you're in journalist mode. All the junk they sling at you out there, life's own scuzzy blizzard of cognitive dissonance: baseball players one day, tantric Buddhists the next. Some of it sticks to you, leads you down another two-month detour from the source of the fictional grail. But that's what they pay me the mediocre bucks for.

Why I Write

STEPHEN WRIGHT

ALL WORK and no play makes Jack a dull boy.
All work and no play makes Jack a dull boy.
All work and no play makes Jack a dyll boy.
Alll work and no play makes Jack a xdull boy.
All work andno play makes jack a dull bit.
All work and no oplay makes Jack a dull boy.
All work and no play makes jack a doll boy.
all work and no play makes jack a dull bot.
Awl work and no play makes Jack a dull Bog.
all work and noplay mokes jack a dfil boy.
All work and no play makes jacka dull boy.
All work and no play makes jackk a dull boy/
all work and no play makes jack a dull boiy.
all work and no play makes Jack a dull boy.
All work and no play makes Jack a dull joy.

all work andno lay makes jack a dull boy.
All work and no playmajk a dull boy.
all work and no play makes jack a dull boiy.
alll work and no playt makes jACK a dull boy.
all work and no play makes kacj a dull noy.
all work and no play makes jack a diull voy.
all work and no playmakes ack a dull boy.
All work and no play makes Jack a dull boy.
All work and no play makes Jack a dull boy.
All work and no play makes Jack a dyll boy.
Alll work and no play makes Jack a xdull boy.
All work andno play makes jack a dull bit.
All work and no oplay makes Jack a dull boy.
All work and no play makes jack a doll boy.
all work and no play makes jack a dull bot.
Awl work and no play makes Jack a dull Bog.
all work and noplay mokes jack a dfil boy.
All work and no play makes jacka dull boy.
All work and no play makes jackk a dull boy/
all work and no play makes jack a dull boiy.
all work and no play makes Jack a dull boy.
All work and no play makes Jack a dull joy.
all work andno lay makes jack a dull boy.
All work and no playmajk a dull boy.
all work and no play makes jack a dull boiy.
alll work and no playt makes jACK a dull boy.
all work and no play makes kacj a dull noy.
all work and no play makes jack a diull voy.
all work and no playmakes ack a dull boy.
All work and no play makes Jack a dull boy.

All work and no play makes Jack a dull boy.
All work and no play makes Jack a dyll boy.
Alll work and no play makes Jack a xdull boy.
All work andno play makes jack a dull bit.
All work and no oplay makes Jack a dull boy.
All work and no play makes jack a doll boy.
all work and no play makes jack a dull bot.
Awl work and no play makes Jack a dull Bog.
all work and noplay mokes jack a dfil boy.
All work and no play makes jacka dull boy.
All work and no play makes jackk a dull boy/
all work and no play makes jack a dull boiy.
all work and no play makes Jack a dull boy.
All work and no play makes Jack a dull joy.
all work andno lay makes jack a dull boy.
All work and no playmajk a dull boy.
all work and no play makes jack a dull boiy.
alll work and no playt makes jACK a dull boy.
all work and no play makes kacj a dull noy.
all work and no play makes jack a diull voy.
all work and no playmakes ack a dull boy.
All work and no play makes Jack a dull boy.
All work and no play makes Jack a dull boy.
All work and no play makes Jack a dyll boy.
Alll work and no play makes Jack a xdull boy.
All work andno play makes jack a dull bit.
All work and no oplay makes Jack a dull boy.
All work and no play makes jack a doll boy.
all work and no play makes jack a dull bot.
Awl work and no play makes Jack a dull Bog.
all work and noplay mokes jack a dfil boy.

All work and no play makes jacka dull boy.
All work and no play makes jackk a dull boy/
all work and no play makes jack a dull boiy.
all work and no play makes Jack a dull boy.
All work and no play makes Jack a dull joy.

Everything Else Falls Away

LEE SMITH

IN THE APPALACHIAN MOUNTAINS, where I grew up, stories come as easy as breathing. Maybe it's something in the water,
or something that seeps out from those storied heights themselves,
rough jagged mountains that held our little town like a jewel in
the palm of a giant hand. But I am more inclined to think it has
to do with who your people are, and how you first hear language.
In my own fortunate case, it was that slow, sweet southern ca-
dence I will always associate with stories; and all those first stories
were told by people who loved me.

My mother, a home-economics teacher from the Eastern
Shore of Virginia, could make a story out of thin air, out of anything — a trip to the drugstore, something somebody said to her in
church. My father liked to drink a little and recite Kipling out
loud. He came from right there, from a large family of storytelling

Democrats who would sit on the porch and place twenty-five-dollar bets on which bird would fly first off a telephone wire. They were all big talkers.

An only child, I heard it all. I was always around the grown-ups, always in the presence of the story.

Every day after school, I walked downtown to my father's dime store, where I got to take care of the dolls, type on a typewriter, count money, and talk to the salesgirls. Viola, back in piece goods, always hugged me; Betty always asked me if I'd been saved yet; and Mildred, my favorite, who wore bright-red spots of rouge on her cheeks and presided over the candy counter, whispered the *craziest* things in my ear. I spent hours upstairs in my father's little office, observing the whole floor through the one-way glass window in my powerful omniscience — *Nobody* can see me! I witnessed not only shoplifting but fights and embraces as well.

Often I'd go to visit my grandaddy in his office at the courthouse across the street, where I'd get the lowdown on who was in jail, who had shot his brother, who was getting married or in debt or out of a job, or had set his house on fire just to collect the insurance money.

Back at home, my mother held forth in the kitchen — we always had company — drinking coffee and smoking Salems and discussing the lives of her friends or the lives of the stars, with equal interest. She and I pored over the *National Enquirer* together. My father read newspapers, magazines, and sometimes history. Although neither of them read novels, they received the Reader's Digest Condensed Books, which I devoured, and they also encouraged me to go to our fledgling library.

This soon got out of hand. I became a voracious and then an obsessive reader; recurrent bouts of pneumonia and tonsillitis gave me plenty of time to indulge my passion. After I was pronounced "sickly," I got to stay home a lot, slathered with a vile salve named Mentholatum, spirit lamp hissing in the corner of my room. I'd read all day and sometimes all night long, under the covers with a flashlight.

But I did not read casually, or for mere entertainment, or for information. What I wanted was to feel all wild and trembly inside, an effect first produced by *The Secret Garden*, which I read maybe twenty times. The only boy I ever loved more than Colin, of *The Secret Garden*, was Johnny Tremaine, in Esther Forbes's book of that title. Other novels that affected me strongly were *Little Women*, especially the part where Beth dies, and *Gone with the Wind*, particularly the scene where Melanie dies. I often imagined I was dying myself, and planned many funerals. I also loved *Marjorie Morningstar*, *A Tree Grows in Brooklyn*, *Heidi*, and books like *Dear and Glorious Physician*, *The Shoes of the Fisherman*, and *Christy*. My all-time favorite was a book about Joan of Arc named *God's Girl*, especially the frontispiece illustration picturing Joan as she knelt and "prayed without ceasing for guidance from God," whose face was depicted overhead, in a thunderstorm. Not only did I love Joan of Arc, I wanted to *be* her.

I was crazy for horses and saints. I read all the Black Stallion books, of course, as well as all the Marguerite Henry books.

"By the way," my mother mentioned to me one day almost casually, while I was being sick in bed and she was straightening my covers, "you know, Marguerite Henry stayed at your grandmother's boardinghouse on Chincoteague Island while she was writing that book."

"What book?" I sat right up.

"*Misty*," Mama said. "Then she came back to write *Sea Star*, and I think the illustrator, Wesley Dennis, stayed there, too. Cousin Jack used to take him out on a boat."

I couldn't believe it! A real writer, a *horse* writer, had walked up the crushed-oyster-shell road where I had gone barefoot, had sat at the big dinner table where I'd eaten fish and corncakes for breakfast; had maybe even swung in the same wicker porch swing I loved.

I wrote a novel on the spot, on eight sheets of my mother's Crane stationery. It featured as its main characters my two favorite people at that time: Adlai Stevenson and Jane Russell. In my novel, they fell in love and then went West together in a covered wagon. Once there, they became — surprisingly — Mormons! Even at that age, I was fixed upon romance, flight, and religion, themes I would return to.

What did my parents think of this strange little girl who had come to them so late in life, when they had become resigned to never having children? Well, because of that fact, they spoiled me rotten and were simply *delighted* by everything I did, everything I showed an interest in. I believe if I had told my mother that I wanted to be, say, an ax murderer, *she* would have said, without blinking an eye, "Well, that's nice, dear," and then gone out to buy me an ax.

Although my parents might *say* — as they did, later — that they wished I would just stop all that writing stuff and marry a surgeon (which is what a daughter really *ought* to do, of course), the fact is that they were so loving that they gave me the confidence, and the *permission*, early on, to do just about anything I wanted to do. Now, decades later, I realize how unusual this was, and how privileged I have been because of it. Now I see this issue — permission to write — as the key one for many women I have worked with in my classes, women who have begun writing later in their lives.

Anyway, in spite of what I have told you, my childhood was not entirely a happy one. No writer's childhood ever is. There was my father's inexplicable sadness; there was my strange uncle Tick; there was a scary little neighborhood "club" we formed, which did bad things. There was a lot of drinking. There were nervous breakdowns, as they called them then, and hospitalizations and long absences and periods of being sent to live with distant relatives. I started dating boys, and almost married one. I got "sent away" to school. Things turned very confusing.

But I kept on writing stories. By the time I got to college, I was writing them, I believe, for the reason I have done so ever since: simply to survive. My belief is that we have only one life, that this is all there is. And I refuse to lead an unexamined life. No matter how painful it may be, I want to know what's going on. So I write fiction the way other people write in their journals.

My husband has been heard to bemoan my lack of self-knowledge. He envisions our respective psyches like this: his is a big room in a factory, brightly lit. He's got uniformed guys in there carrying clipboards and constantly working on all his problems, checking gauges and levels, in day and night shifts. He's always monitoring their work, reading their reports. He sees *my* mind, by contrast, as a dark forest with no path, where huge beasts loom up at you suddenly out of the night and then disappear, only to return again and again and again.

Maybe so. But when I read what I've written, I know exactly what those beasts are.

In 1980, for instance, I wrote a novel named *Black Mountain Breakdown*, about a girl named Crystal Spangler, who is so busy fitting herself into others' images of her (first fulfilling her mother's beauty-queen dreams, then altering her image to suit the various men in her life) that she loses her own true self and finally ends up paralyzed: "Crystal just lies up there in that room every day, with her bed turned catty-corner so she could look out the window and see Lorene's climbing rambler rose in full bloom on the trellis if she would turn her head. But she won't. She won't lift a finger. She just lies there. Everybody in town takes a fancy to it." The townsfolk feed her Jell-O, brush her hair, read *Reader's Digest* out loud to her. The most terrifying aspect of her condition is that "Crystal is happy . . . as outside her window the seasons come and go and the colors change on the mountain." When I wrote that, I was in a marriage that should have ended years earlier, something I'd been unable to face or even admit; later, reading these words over, I finally understood how I'd felt during the last part of that marriage. I was able then to deal with its inevitable ending, and move on with my life.

No matter what I may *think* I am writing about at any given time — even majorettes in Alabama, even a gruesome long-ago murder, or country music — I have come to understand that it is all, finally, about me, often in some complicated way I won't come to understand until years later. But then it will be there for me to read, and I *will* understand it, and even if I don't know who I am now, I will surely have a record of who I was then.

Writing is also my addiction, for the moment when I am writing fiction is that moment when I am most intensely alive. This "aliveness" does not seem to be mental, or not exactly. I am certainly not *thinking* while I write. Whatever I'm doing is almost the opposite of thinking. Especially during the prewriting phase, when I am simply making up the story and imagining its characters, and during the first couple of drafts, I feel a dangerous, exhilarating sense that anything can happen.

It reminds me of a woman I interviewed in eastern Kentucky several years ago when I was writing a novel about serpent-handling believers. An hour earlier, I had seen her lift a double handful of copperheads high in the air during a religious service. Now we faced each other across a little formica table in a fast-food restaurant, drinking Cokes and eating fries. I asked the obvious: "Why do you do this, when it's so dangerous? You could die any time." She merely smiled at me, a beautiful, generous smile without a trace of irony.

"Honey," she began, "I do it out of an intense desire for holiness." She smiled at me again while that sank in. "And I'll tell you something else, too. When you've held the serpent in your hands, the whole world kind of takes on an edge for you."

I could see that. For I had once been the girl who embarrassed her mother so much by rededicating her life over and over at various revivals, coming home dripping wet from total immersions in those stand-up pools from Sears that they set up in the little tents behind the big tents, or simply in the fast-flowing creeks that rushed down the mountainsides.

And the feeling I get when I'm writing intensely is much the same.

For me, writing is a physical joy. It is almost sexual — not the moment of fulfillment, but the moment when you open the door to the room where your lover is waiting, and everything else falls away.

It *does* fall away, too. For the time of the writing, I am nobody. Nobody at all. I am a conduit, nothing but a way for the story to come to the page. Oh, but I am terribly alive then, too, though I say I am no one at all; my every sense is keen and quivering. I can smell the bacon cooking downstairs in my grandmother's kitchen that winter morning in 1952, I can feel the cold linoleum floor under my bare feet as I run down the hall, I can see the bright-blue squares of the kitchen wallpaper, bunches of cherries alternating with little floral bouquets. Sun shines through the frost on the windows, almost blinding me; my granddaddy's Lucky Strike cigarette smoke still hangs in the air, lazy blue, though he is already up and gone, has walked the bridge across the river to the old stone courthouse where he will work all day long as county treasurer. I love my granddaddy, who always wears a dark-blue suit and has a figure like Humpty Dumpty's. I do not so much love my grandmother, who tells me not to be a tomboy and not to start sentences with "me and Martha." "Say, 'Martha and I,'" she directs, moistening her lips with her tongue in a way I hate. I wish my mother would get out of the hospital so I could go home. I don't see why I can't stay with Daddy, anyway. I could make us peanut butter sandwiches for dinner, and cut the crusts off.

See what I mean? I am *there* now, and I want to stay there. I hate to leave that kitchen and come back to this essay. Writing an essay is like pulling teeth, compared to writing fiction. It is an intellectual exercise rather than a sensory experience.

All my senses are involved when I am writing fiction, but it is *hearing* that is most acute. This has always been true. I can see everything in the story, of course — I have to see that kitchen in order to walk through it, and the icy river in order to get my grandfather across the bridge. I make a lot of maps before I start writing, scotch-taping them up on the wall. But I am not a visual person in real life. I never know how high to hang pictures, for instance, or where the furniture should go. None of my clothes match. It was *words* I loved first, remember, words and sentences and music and stories, the voice that comes out of the dark when you're almost asleep, sitting in somebody's lap on somebody's porch, trying to keep your eyes open long enough to hear the end of the story.

So a story always comes to me in a human voice, speaking not exactly into my ear but somewhere deep inside me. If I am writing from a first-person point of view, it is always the voice of the person who is telling the story. If I am writing from a third-person point of view, it is simply the voice of the story itself. Sometimes this voice is slow and pondering, or tentative and unsure. Sometimes it is flat and reportorial: just the facts, ma'am. Sometimes it's giggly, gossipy, intimate — a tale told over a Coke and a cigarette during a work break at the Piggly Wiggly. Sometimes it's sad, a long, wailing lament, telling and retelling again and again how he done me wrong. It can be furious or vengeful: "I hated him from the moment I first laid eyes on him, hated him instinctively, as if I knew somehow what he would do to our family. . . ." It can be a meditative, authoritative voice, told as if from the distant past or from a great and somehow definitive distance (I confess that ever since we moved into this old house where I work in an upstairs study looking out over the town, this has happened more frequently!).

Most thrilling, of course, is when it is a first-person voice telling a story of real urgency. At these times, all I have to do is *keep up*; I become a stenographer, a court secretary, a tape recorder. My biggest job is making sure that I have several uninterrupted hours whenever I sit down to write, so this can happen. Whenever a story like this is in progress, it is so exciting that I will do almost anything to get those hours: break appointments, call in sick, tell lies. I become a person on drugs, somebody in the throes of a passionate affair. I'll do anything to get there, to make it happen again. I know I can't ignore the voice, or waste it. I may be a fool, but I'm not *that kind* of fool.

Since the writing of fiction is such a physical and personal process for me, I have to write in longhand, still. I have to write with a pen or pencil on a legal pad. I can't have anything mechanical between my body and the page. Later, I'll type it on my little typewriter again and again and again, as I revise. I buy these ninety-nine-dollar typewriters three at a time from Home Depot and run through them like crazy. I always keep a couple stockpiled; I'm terrified that they'll quit making them. Later, I will get somebody who's a better typist than I am to put it on a disk, for publishers that expect to get it that way.

Here's what I don't understand about composing on a computer: I'm really messy when I write, and often jot down three or four words before I hit upon the right one. So I mark all the others out and go on writing, but I want to *keep* them all, all those words I thought about first and then discarded. I want to keep that paragraph of description I marked out, and that earlier section about how Ray drowned the dog when he was nine, because I might change my mind later on. The story, at this point, is organic, living, changing; anything can still happen, and probably will. This is true up until the very moment when I put it into its little coffin, usually an old typewriter-paper box, and mail it off. Then it's dead, they're all dead, all those people who have been my familiars, who have lived under my skin for weeks and months or years, and I am no longer writer, but murderer and mourner, more alone in the world.

Writing is a source of strength for me, too. I had barely begun a novel named *Fair and Tender Ladies* — intended as an honest account and a justification, really, of the lives of so many of the resourceful mountain women I'd grown up among, women whose plain and home-centered lives are not much valued in the world at large — when my beloved mother went into her last illness, a long and drawn-out sequence of falls, emphysema, and finally heart failure. This period coincided with another catastrophic illness in our family; I spent two years sitting by hospital beds. I don't know what I would have done if I hadn't been writing that novel. I worked on it a bit every day; it was like an open door to another world, another place for me to be for a little while.

Its heroine, Ivy Rowe, grew stronger and stronger the more I needed her. Every terrible thing in the world happened to her — extreme poverty, too many children, heartbreak, illness, the death of a child — but she could take it. She hung in there, so I did, too. Ivy made sense of *her* life through writing a constant stream of letters, to her children, to her friends, to her sisters — especially to her favorite sister, Silvaney, even though she had died young and would never read most of them. Near the novel's end, Ivy burns all her letters, and it is finally my *own* voice as well as hers that concludes:

> I gathered them up and took them back to the firepit, where we used to lay the kettle to boil our clothes when I was a girl, it has taken me several trips as I move so slow now. I cleared out the snow in the firepit and took my big old kitchen matches out there and burned the letters every one. Now and then I would stop and look all around, but you know how quiet the land lies in the snow. . . . The clouds hung low and dark and puffy. My breath hung in the air. The smoke from the burning letters rose and was lost in the clouds. . . . With every one I burned, my soul grew lighter, lighter, as if it rose too with

the smoke. And I was not even cold, long as I'd been out there. For I came to understand something in that moment which I had never understood in all these years.

Those letters didn't mean anything.
Not to the dead girl, Silvaney, of course — *nor to me.*
Nor had they ever.
It was the *writing* of them that signified.

The Nature of the Fun

DAVID FOSTER WALLACE

THE BEST METAPHOR I know of for being a fiction writer is in Don DeLillo's *Mao II*, where he describes a book-in-progress as a kind of hideously damaged infant that follows the writer around, forever crawling after the writer (dragging itself across the floors of restaurants where the writer's trying to eat, appearing at the foot of the bed first thing in the morning, etc.), hideously defective, hydrocephalic and noseless and flipper-armed and incontinent and retarded and dribbling cerebro-spinal fluid out of its mouth as it mewls and blurbles and cries out to the writer, wanting love, wanting the very thing its hideousness guarantees it'll get: the writer's complete attention.

The damaged-infant trope is perfect because it captures the mix of repulsion and love the fiction writer feels for something he's working on. The fiction always comes out so horrifically defective, so hideous a betrayal of all your hopes for it — a cruel and repellent caricature of the perfection of its conception — yes, understand: grotesque because *imperfect*. And yet it's yours, the infant is, it's *you*, and you love it and dandle it and wipe the cerebrospinal fluid off its slack chin with the cuff of the only clean shirt you have left (you have only one clean shirt left because you haven't done laundry in like three weeks because finally this one chapter or character seems like it's finally trembling on the edge of coming together and working and you're terrified to spend any time on anything other than working on it because if you look away for a second you'll lose it, dooming the whole infant to continued hideousness). And so you love the damaged infant and pity it and care for it; but also you hate it — *hate it* — because it's deformed, repellent, because something grotesque has happened to it in the parturition from head to page; hate it because its deformity is *your* deformity (since if you were a better fiction writer your infant would of course look like one of those babies in catalog ads for infant wear, perfect and pink and cerebro-spinally continent) and its every hideous incontinent breath is a devastating indictment of *you*, on all levels . . . and so you want it dead, even as you dote on it and wipe it and dandle it and sometimes even apply CPR when it seems like its own grotesqueness has blocked its breath and it might die altogether.

The whole thing's all very messed up and sad, but simultaneously it's also tender and moving and noble and cool — it's a genuine *relationship*, of a sort — and even at the height of its hideousness the damaged infant somehow touches and awakens what you suspect are some of the very best parts of you: maternal parts, dark ones. You love your infant very much. And you want others to love it, too, when the time finally comes for the damaged infant to go out and face the world.

So you're in a bit of a dicey position: you love the infant and you want others to love it, but that means that you hope others won't see it *correctly*. You want to sort of fool people; you want them to see as perfect what you in your heart know is a betrayal of all perfection.

Or else you don't want to fool these people; what you want is you want them to see and love a lovely, miraculous, perfect, already infant and to be *right*, *correct*, in what they see and feel. You want to be terribly wrong, you want the damaged infant's hideousness to turn out to have been nothing but your own weird delusion or hallucination. But that'd mean you were crazy; you have seen, been stalked by, and recoiled from hideous deformities that in fact (others persuade you) aren't there at all. Meaning you're at least a couple of fries short of a Happy Meal, surely. But worse: it'd also mean you saw and despised hideousness in a thing *you* made (and love), in your spawn and in certain ways, *you*. And this last, best hope, this'd represent something way worse than just very bad parenting; it'd be a terrible kind of self-assault, almost self-torture. But that's still what you most want: to be completely, insanely, suicidally wrong.

But it's still all a lot of fun. Don't get me wrong. As to the nature of that fun, I keep remembering this strange little story I heard in Sunday school when I was about the size of a fire hydrant. It takes place in China or Korea or someplace like that. It seems there is this old farmer outside a village in the hill country who worked his farm with only his son and his beloved horse. One day the horse, who was not only beloved but vital to the labor-intensive work on the farm, picked the lock on his corral or whatever and ran off into the hills. All the old farmer's friends came around to exclaim what bad luck this was. The farmer only shrugged and said, "Good luck, bad luck, who knows?" A couple days later the beloved horse returned from the hills in the company of a whole priceless herd of wild horses, and the farmer's friends all come around to congratulate him on what good luck the horse's escape turned out to be. "Good luck, bad luck, who knows?" is all the farmer says in reply, shrugging. The farmer now strikes me as a bit Yiddish-sounding for an old Chinese farmer, but this is how I remember it. But so the farmer and his son set about breaking the wild horses, and one of the horses bucks the son off his back with such wild force that the son breaks his leg. And here come the friends to commiserate with the farmer and curse the bad luck that ever brought these accursed wild horses onto his farm. The old farmer just shrugs and says, "Good luck, bad luck, who knows?" A few days later the Imperial Sino-Korean Army or something like that comes marching through the village, conscripting every able-bodied male between like ten and sixty for cannon-fodder for some hideously bloody conflict that's apparently brewing, but when they see the son's broken leg, they let him off on some sort of feudal 4F, and instead of getting shanghaied the son stays on the farm with the old farmer. Good luck? Bad luck?

This is the sort of parabolic straw you cling to as you struggle with the issue of fun, as a writer. In the beginning, when you first start out trying to write fiction, the whole endeavor's about fun. You don't expect anybody else to read it. You're writing almost wholly to get yourself off. To enable your own fantasies and deviant logics and to escape or transform parts of yourself you don't like. And it works — and it's terrific fun. Then, if you have good luck and people seem to like what you do, and you actually start to get paid for it and get to see your stuff professionally typeset and bound and blurbed and reviewed and even (once) being read on the A.M. subway by a pretty girl you don't even know, it seems to make it even *more* fun. For a while. Then things start to get complicated and confusing, not to mention scary. Now you feel like you're writing for other people, or at least you hope so. You're no longer writing just to get yourself off, which — since any kind of masturbation is lonely and hollow — is probably good. But what replaces the onanistic motive? You've found you very much enjoy having your writing liked by people, and you find you're extremely keen to have people like the new stuff you're doing. The motive of pure personal fun starts to get supplanted by the motive of being liked, of having pretty people you don't know like you and admire you and think you're a good writer. Onanism gives way to attempted seduction, as a motive. Now, attempted seduction is hard work, and its fun is offset by a terrible fear of rejection. Whatever "ego" means, your ego has now gotten into the game. Or maybe "vanity" is a better word. Because you notice that a good deal of your writing has now become basically showing off, trying to get people to think you're good. This is understandable. You have a great deal of yourself on the line, now, writing — your vanity is at stake. You discover a tricky thing about fiction writing: a certain amount of vanity is necessary to be able to do it all, but any vanity above that certain amount is lethal. At some point you find that 90-plus percent of the stuff you're writing is motivated and informed by an overwhelming need to be liked. This results in shitty fiction. And the shitty work must get fed to the wastebasket, less because of any sort of artistic integrity than simply because shitty work will cause you to be disliked. At this point in the evolution of writerly fun, the very thing that's always motivated you to write is now also what's motivating you to feed your writing to the wastebasket. This is a paradox and a kind of double bind, and it can keep you stuck inside yourself for months or even years, during which period you wail and gnash and rue your bad luck and wonder bitterly where all the *fun* of the thing could have gone.

The smart thing to say, I think, is that the way out of this bind is to work your way somehow back to your original motivation — fun. And if you can find your way back to fun, you will find that the hideously unfortunate double bind of the late vain period turns out really to have been good luck for you. Because the fun you work back to has been transfigured by the extreme unpleasantness of vanity and fear, an unpleasantness you're now so anxious to avoid that the fun you rediscover is a way fuller and more large-hearted kind of fun. It has something to do with Work as Play. Or with the discovery that disciplined fun is more fun than impulsive or hedonistic fun. Or with figuring out that not all paradoxes have to be paralyzing. Under fun's new administration, writing fiction becomes a way to go deep inside yourself and illuminate precisely the stuff you don't want to see or let anyone else see, and this stuff usually turns out (paradoxically) to be precisely the stuff all writers and readers everywhere share and respond to, feel. Fiction becomes a weird way to countenance yourself and to tell the truth instead of being a way to escape yourself or present yourself in a way you figure you will be maximally likable. This process is complicated and confusing and scary, and also hard work, but it turns out to be the best fun there is.

The fact that you can now sustain the fun of writing only by confronting the very same unfun parts of yourself you'd first used writing to avoid or disguise is another paradox, but this one isn't any kind of bind at all. What it is is a gift, a kind of miracle, and compared to it the rewards of strangers' affection is as dust, lint.

Why I Write, or Not

JIM HARRISON

Standing outside the Metropolitan Museum in New York several years ago, feeling sodden and perplexed over the Goya show, I ran into an old friend, the poet Charles Simic, whom I hadn't seen in twenty years. Among other things that we talked about, he said, "I thought I'd understand everything by now, but I don't," and I think I replied, "We know a great deal but not very much."

I'm not saying that we throw in the towel on our rational mind, one that we only had two fingers on in the first place, but with age, the processes of my own art seem a great deal more immutable and inexplicable to me. For instance, even without my eyes closed, specific ideas usually carry an equally specific visual image for me. The act of writing is a boy hoeing a field of corn on a hot day, able to see either a woodlot or, more often, an immense forest where he'd rather be. This is uncomplicated, almost banal. He has to hoe the corn in order to be allowed to reach his beloved forest. This can be easily extrapolated into the writer as a small god who has forty acres as a birthright in which to reinvent the world. He cultivates this world, but then there is always something vast and unreachable beyond his grasp, whether it's the forest, the ocean, or the implausible ten million citizens of New York or Paris. While he hoes or writes, he whirls toward the future at a rate that with age becomes quite incomprehensible. He leaves a trail of books, but he really marks the passage of time by the series of hunting dogs he's left behind. His negative capability has made the world grow larger rather than shrink, and not a single easy answer has survived the passing of years.

It is more comic than melancholy because the presumptions are so immense. No matter how much you've read, something has been left out that you aim to fill in yourself. This takes a great deal of hubris and frequently a measure of stupidity. Our large family read widely if indiscriminately, the movie theater in our small town in northern Michigan changing features only once a week. I began with the usual Horatio Alger, Zane Grey, Hardy Boys flotsam, graduated to my father's passion for literate historical novels, especially those of Kenneth Roberts, Hervey Allen, and Walter Edmonds, and then also to his taste for (he was an agriculturist) Hamlin Garland and Sherwood Anderson and Erskine Caldwell, before continuing on my own so that by nineteen my obsessive favorites included Dostoyevski, Whitman, Yeats, Kierkegaard, Joyce, Rimbaud, Apollinaire, Henry Miller, and Faulkner. Such a list might very well lead an intelligent soul to keep his mouth shut, but then a curious arrogance has always been the breastplate of a young writer's armor. At this stage humility is a hobble you can scarcely afford. The only fuel the ego receives is interior. You might wander around in a thunderstorm, hiding out and repeating *Non serviam*, but then no one has asked you to do anything, and no one is looking for you, least of all those whom you have tormented with your postures.

Despite early forays to New York, Boston, and San Francisco, my work is preoccupied with rural life and the natural world. I must say that I don't see any special virtue to this. You are pretty much stuck with what you know, and Peter Matthiessen with his obsessive preoccupation with the natural world balances nicely with a taste for the more urbane James Salter or Don DeLillo. It is the artfulness of the prose and construct I'm looking for, not someone's fungoid wisdom. Good writers seem to know that we are permanently inconsolable.

It is the mystery of personality that seizes me, the infinite variety of human behavior that thumbs its nose at popular psychologisms. Even our dreams seem to wish to create new characters as surely as we do in our fictions, and our creation of our own personalities is most often a fictive event. In creating an environment for certain of my characters, I often find myself trying to create an environment for my own soul. The perception of reality grows until it is an accretion of the perceptions of all creatures. It is a daily struggle against the habituation and conditioning that bind us and suffocate us, destroying the fascinating perceptions that characterize the best writing. You continue under the willful illusion that the world is undescribed, or else you need not exist, and you never quite tire of the bittersweet mayhem of human behavior.

Except, of course, for the fatigue brought on by our collective behavior, both political and economic, the moral hysteria we are currently sunken in. Last May without an inkling I found myself saying in a French interview that we are becoming a Fascist Disneyland. This is seeping into our fiction and poetry in the form of a new Victorianism wherein a mawkish sincerity is the highest value. At one point I thought it was simply the way academia had subsumed serious fiction and poetry, but now it seems that academia and the small presses are the only barriers against totally market-driven work, despite the other obvious middling shortcomings of the M.F.A. pyramid schema, a sad breeder of middling expectations and large disappointments.

The national mood that affects our work is naturally more complicated. An English anthropologist, Mary Douglas, once said, "The more that society is vested with power, the more it despises the organic processes on which it rests." Each year we become more like Europe, with cultural rigidity typical of an increasing population that has doubled in my own lifetime. Otherness, the primal core of our lives, the unmediated aspects of our existence, our lives and loves and deaths, the rituals we have used to frame our existence for thousands of years, can't hold up and haven't under the sodden blanket of the collective media, whether television or the Internet. There is the darkly comic vision of this media-fueled cultural blender increasing in size and power until that is all there is. A blender as big as Ohio, spewing the trash, chatter, and clutter we're all familiar with. Art is confused and smothered by the art market, literature is seen as an arm of publishing rather than vice versa. Animals are what you see in the zoos within the zoos of our lives. Certain eco-Nazis appear to think that all animals still surviving in the wild, especially grizzlies and wolves, require telemetric devices. Like politics, the *rodentia* will thrive. The majority of our population that eats beef, pork, and chicken has never known an actual cow, pig, or hen. Times change, as our parents told us, and are not the less fascinating for the colors of the grotesque.

We paint our lives as we write our work, and I'm reminded of Whitman's statement that a poet must "move wild laughter in the throat of death." I've always had a somewhat childish obsession with thickets, and I suspect this shows in my work. I like a specific density in fiction and poetry, feeling that the easily perceived is almost always valueless. I often have wondered if my somewhat Pleistocene fixation with thickets, niches, and lairs may have had its origin in the childhood trauma of being blinded in one eye, but then so what? The explanation is flotsam. It is all so wonderfully random, accidental, just as hundreds since my youth have thought my appearance to be Native American, though those genes seem unlikely in my family. We have chosen to be outcasts, and they didn't, so the identification is inappropriate. There is also the suspicion that the craving for identity is the cause of the literary disease of xenophobia. Since nearly everyone is dislocated, including writers within our current critical diaspora, the staking out, lauding, and defense of territories, an otiose form of regionalism, is even more absurd. Of course literary rages, fads, events, and quarrels don't age any better than Beaujolais or the "skinless, boneless chicken breasts" that are evidently the prime meat of our time. Metaphorically, writers are better off eating the elephant's asshole, stewed thirty-three hours with hot chilies, that I partook of in Tanzania way back when.

I used to think I was becoming quadra-schizoid by writing poetry, fiction, essays, and screenplays, but then since I don't teach, I've always had a hand in all of those forms to make a living. We would be nothing without the good teachers in our lives, but I never had any temperament for it, as universities are invariably in locales where I couldn't survive due to my lifelong claustrophobia.

Poetry comes when it will, and I've never had any idea of how to cause it. Way back during the T'ang Dynasty, Wang Wei, a phenomenal poet, said, "Who knows what causes the opening or closing of the door?" There has always been a tendency among poets in slack periods to imitate their own best efforts, but this is embarrassingly obvious to their readers. It's a bit like raping your own brain, or trying to invent a convincing sexual fantasy only to have the phone ring and it's your mother, who wonders why you're still a "bohemian" at age fifty-nine. The actual muse is the least civil woman in the history of earth. She prefers to sleep with you when you're a river rather than a mud puddle.

I wrote my first sequence of novellas in the late seventies and had some difficulty getting them published, as "no one" was writing them in those days. My own models were Isak Dinesen and Katherine Anne Porter in my search for an intermediate form. I've never been able to write a short story, which used to make me a bit nervous, as magazines kept prattling that this was the "age of the short story." I became less nervous when it occurred to me that these selfsame magazines couldn't very well publish novels or novellas, though the New Yorker did publish my "The Woman Lit by Fireflies" and Esquire printed the novella "Legends of the Fall" in its entirety. A publisher who turned the latter down suggested I increase its mere hundred pages to five hundred and then we'd have a best-seller, no matter that, unchanged, it has eventually sold quite well for twenty years. Publishers naturally have the same yearning for instant gratification as dope addicts, congressmen, and car dealers. Now, under corporate and chain-store dominance, they appear to be paddleless up a terribly real shit creek.

Novels seem to take care of themselves if you offer them up an appropriate amount of time. I've never written one without first thinking about it for years. This is probably a peculiar method, but I can't function otherwise. I just did a year's research for the second section of a novel and ended up using very little. This is what the film business aptly calls "back story," without the knowledge of which it is difficult to proceed. If a woman character is thirty-seven, you still have to figure out the nature of her personality when she was a child, even if you have no intention of using that.

I've also written more screenplays than I should have, but then I've been fascinated by movies since I was a child. Admittedly, this fascination has never been very mainstream, which has caused me problems when looking for work. I doubt if there are proportionately any more first-rate novels than good movies in a particular year, but given the intelligentsia's scorn of Hollywood, this is not an acceptable idea. I admit there is a cynicism and perfidy in Hollywood that almost approach those of Washington and are probably equal to those in book publishing, but I have also noted evidence that some of the loathing for Hollywood is a veiled form of anti-Semitism and being a mixture of Swede-Irish-English, I can say this without paranoia.

I suppose the main problem in screenwriting is that you're separated from the possible director until later in the series of drafts. This is a waste of time and money, especially since you have a good idea of a suitable director from the inception of the story. Another pronounced difficulty is that film-school graduates are definitely short on the varieties of human experience in favor of cinematic technology. Despite the fact that very bright movies tend to do well, there is a relentless and collective effort to "dumb down" the story. There is always the fear-maddened search on the part of film executives for a reliable formula story line, with inevitably sad results. On the plus side, no matter the whining, there always has been more oxygen in the West. Even Bill Gates wouldn't have done very well in Connecticut or Gotham. To be even as peripherally involved in the film business as I am, you have to have a taste for insanity and vulgarity, insecurity, hideous disappointments, spates of beauty, being fired over and over, and very good pay. It is usually a shuddering elevator far above ground, but I prefer it to intense domesticity. Yeats used to say that the hearth killed more poets than alcohol.

I've recently had the uncomfortable feeling that despite my rather harsh Calvinist will, I've had less control over the trajectory of my life than I had presumed. I suppose it's because of the semi-religious nature of the original period of the calling. Without going into the anthropological aspects, the beginning of the calling when I was in my early teens was similar to a seizure. I had abruptly given up on organized religion, and I suspect that all of that somewhat hormonal fervor merely transferred itself to what I still think of as Art, whether painting, music, poetry, sculpture, or fiction. Keats and Modigliani seemed excellent models for a life! The fact that neither of them lasted very long is a nominal consideration for a teenager. If you spend hours and hours listening to Stravinsky while reading Rimbaud and Joyce, you are fueling a trajectory that is inevitably out of immediate control. If you reread all of Dostoyevski on Grove Street in New York City in a seven-dollar-a-week room with only an air vent for a window, you are permanently at age nineteen changing the nature of your mind. In your self-drama you are building an intractably wild mind that you'll have to live with.

Of course, in geological terms we all have the same measure of immortality. The heartbeat that is your own, that you occasionally hear while turning over in bed in a cramped position, doesn't last very long. The immediate noise your book might make is woefully impermanent, and self-importance is invariably an anchor. In immediate literary history, say the last fifty years, by reading lists of prizes and remembering vaunted reputations, you see how even the grandest fame is usually written on water. News magazines for years liked to refer to Faulkner as Old Mister Cornpone; when

I was a teenager, he was far less favored than James Gould Cozzens. Finally, what happens to your work is not your concern. Thinking about it gives your soul cramps that resemble amoebic dysentery.

The mail over the years has brought me thousands of manuscripts and galleys and letters from young writers. It is possible to drown in paper, but even more dangerous is the nasty mood of feeling put-upon. Other than recommending quantities of red wine and garlic, I am without advice. The closest I can come is, Don't do it unless you're willing to give up your entire life. Despite the human-potential movement, there is no room for much else. And Einstein was on the money when he said that he had no admiration for scientists who selected thin pieces of board and drove countless holes in them. You should always want your work to be better than your capabilities, as settling for less is a form of artistic death.

I'd also rather err on the side of creating humans as more than they are rather than less. There is a whining penchant for lifting the bandage, for forgetting that a body is much more than its collective wounds. In any culture, art and literature seem terribly fragile, but we should remember that they always outlive the culture. In an age of extraordinary venality such as our own, when the government is only a facilitator of commerce, they come under a great deal of general contempt, as if every single soul must become bung fodder for greed. But then we are nature, too, and historically art and literature are as natural as the migration of birds or the inevitable collision of love and death.

The Wolf in the Tall Grass

MARY GAITSKILL

Why do I write?

1. *To satisfy a basic, fundamental need.* I think all people have this need. It's why children like to draw pictures of houses, animals, and Mom; it's an affirmation of their presence in the corporeal world. You come into life, and life gives you everything your senses can bear: broad currents of animal feeling running along-side the particularity of thought. Sunlight, stars, colors, smells, sounds. Tender things, sweet, temperate things, harsh, freezing, hot, and salty things. All the different expressions on people's faces and in their voices. For years, everything just pours into you, and all you can do is gurgle or scream until finally one day you can sit up and hold your crayon and draw your picture and thus shout back, Yes! I hear! I see! I feel! This is what it's like! It's dynamic

creation and pure, delighted receptivity happening on the same field, a great call and response.

This is true even when the pictures describe horrible, even deadly events; the children at Auschwitz drew pictures. The word *delighted* may not apply in situations like that, but the fact that children draw pictures in such unspeakable circumstances shows the depth of the need to represent. Even when it's about pain and horror, it's still a powerful act to say, Yes, I see. I feel. I hear. This is what it's like. To do so asserts a fundamental, even fierce tenacity that a person needs to survive.

When I learned to write, at the age of six, the first thing I did was write a story. It was about blue jays that courted and married. They did things real birds don't do; I made it up, and in doing so I went from basic need to something more complicated.

2. *To give form to the things we can sense but not see.* You walk into the living room where your father is lying on the couch, listening to music. You are small, so he doesn't hear or see you. His face is reacting to the music, and his expression is soft, abstract, intensely inward. It is also pained. It is an expression that you have never seen. Then he sees you and smiles, but the music still fills the room with that other expression. Another time, walking on the street, you pass a stranger whose face arrests you; in her eyes you see something that makes you think of her alone in a tenement eating a cold-cut sandwich. You think of her missing someone she once loved who didn't love her. The woman has told you something with her eyes, and you've felt it; you don't know what it is, but you have a picture of it anyway. And it's something much more than what you saw physically. A friend of mine once told me that he still remembers seeing, as a young boy, his camp counselor come out of a cabin with an expression on his face that made

my friend start to cry. It wasn't because the expression was so sad; it was because it was filled with such hope and enthusiasm, which my friend imagined becoming increasingly damaged, worn, and brittle. He didn't know that to be true; he made it up.

When I was eleven, I wrote a story about a man who woke up in total darkness. He had no idea where he was, and he was very afraid. He tried to decide if he should sit and wait for it to get light or if he should move forward. After some thought, he decided to take a step forward, and he fell down his basement stairs. It was a kid's Twilight Zone story about a sleepwalker, but it was also about what I could sense and not see: something very ordinary— the basement stairs — becomes a big, mystic problem and then the cause of a cartoon pratfall.

As an adult, I once wrote a story about a man who discovers that his daughter has written about him in a highly personal way for a women's magazine. She hasn't told him about it; he hears about it by chance. It's a ridiculous and painful situation, for this father and daughter have had a miserable relationship that they've never discussed, and now here she is discussing it publicly, in "ghastly talk-show language." The very ordinary thing — the magazine — becomes a vehicle for the awful, complex darkness into which the man falls. Except that this darkness is very rich. The daughter uses language that is banal and cloying, but she is expressing powerful feelings. Ironically, the very strangeness and indirectness of his discovery of the article allow him to take in what she says in a way that he might not have done if he had been directly approached. His first reaction is anger, but slowly, almost unconsciously, he begins to feel things he still can't see — about his daughter and about himself.

Nabokov, in his published lectures on literature, said that literature was born the day a boy came running out of the undergrowth yelling Wolf, wolf, and there was no wolf: "Between the wolf in the tall grass and the wolf in the tall story, there is a shimmering go-between. That go-between, that prism, is the art of literature." I'm not sure I understand exactly what he meant, but I think it's partly this: stories mimic life like certain insects mimic leaves and twigs. Stories are about all the things that might've, could've, or would've happened, encrowded around and giving density and shape to undeniable physical events and phenomena. They are the rich, unseen underlayer of the most ordinary moments. I get great satisfaction from plunging my hands into that underlayer.

3. *To feel important, in the simplest egotistical sense.* This motivation may not seem to have much to do with what I wrote above, but it does. Strong thoughts and feelings about what you see and feel require a distinct point of view and an ego. If you are frequently told that your point of view is worthless, invalid, or crazy, your ego will get really insulted. It will sulk like a teenager hunched in her room muttering, "No one ever listens. No one cares. One day, they'll see!" To make them all see — i.e., see how important I am — was once a big part of why I wrote stories. As a motivation, it's embarrassing, it's base, and it smells bad, but it's also an angry little engine that could. It will fight like hell to keep your point of view from being snatched away, or demeaned, fighting even when there's no apparent threat. The only problem is, the more your ego fights, the smaller your point of view gets. For a while, I needed to take great pains to make myself feel safe, to the point of extreme social isolation, so I wouldn't feel like I had to fight. The angry engine quieted down a bit, and I began to learn about other points of view.

4. To reveal and restore things that I feel might be ignored or disregarded. I was once in a coffee shop eating breakfast alone when I noticed a woman standing and talking to a table of people. She was young but prematurely aged, with badly dyed hair and lined skin. She was smiling and joking, but her body had a collapsed, defeated posture that looked deeply habitual. Her spine was curled, her head was slightly receded, and her shoulders were pulled down in a static flinch. She expressed herself loudly and crudely, but also diffidently. She talked like she was a joke. But there was something else to her, something pushing up against the defeat, a sweet, tough, humorous vitality that I could almost see running up her center. I realized that if I hadn't looked closely, I would not have really seen this woman, that I would not have seen what was most human and lively in her. I wondered how many people saw it, or even if she herself saw it. I thought of her when I wrote about a character named Patty, an aggressively promiscuous girl with a "nasty sense of humor" who repeatedly sets herself up to be rejected and brutalized. To me the character is affecting, not because she is a victim, but because her victimization comes about from her terribly misguided efforts to assert herself — from the sweet, tough, humorous vitality that goes unrecognized even by her and is grossly misused. The male character who shares the story with her, John, is someone who rather blindly mistreats her and realizes too late that he's sorry for doing so. His attempts to make amends to a stranger are so ham-fisted and inappropriate that they look like a grotesque come-on. The story ends in apparent futility and embarrassment. But John's bumbling effort harbors a very pure impulse: he is finally attempting to confront his own cruelty and to forgive himself for it. Even if he doesn't know it, the attempt is like a tiny bud of sorrow and compassion in him, and because it is so small and new, it's easily missed.

That kind of small, new, unrecognized thing is very tender to me, and I hate it when it gets ignored or mistaken for something ugly. I want to acknowledge and nurture it, but I usually leave it very small in the stories. I do that because I think part of the human puzzle is in the delicacy of those moments or phenomena, contrasted with the ignorance and lack of feeling we are subject to.

5. *To communicate.* To write about the kind of moments I've described above and to have people read what I've written and understand it is deeply satisfying. To read well is an act of dynamic receptivity that creates a profound sense of exchange, and I like being on both ends of it. In Saul Bellow's early novel *The Victim*, he describes his beleaguered protagonist on the way to a funeral parlor where his young nephew's body is being prepared for burial. He is walking through a working-class neighborhood:

> The heat of the pavement penetrated his soles and he felt it in the very bones of his feet. In a long, black peninsular yard a row of scratchy bushes grew, dead green. The walls were flaming coarsely, and each thing — the moping bushes, the face of a woman appearing at a screen, a heap of melons before a grocery — came to him as though raised to a new power and given another quality by the air; and the colors, granular and bloody, black, green, blue, quivered like gases over the steady baselines of shadow. The open door of the grocery was like the entrance to a cave or mine; the cans shone like embedded rocks.

This passage is a raw beauty (one among many in this book) that is as important as anything that happens in the book's plot. It opens life up down to the pit; when I read that, I can't ignore how extraordinary it is to be alive.

6. *To integrate; to love.* One of Nabokov's early novels, *Laughter in the Dark,* has an apparently simple, almost hackneyed plot: a foolish, wealthy, middle-aged man (Albinus) falls in love with a vulgar, heartless sixteen-year-old girl (Margot). She and her lover, Rex, proceed to destroy Albinus and his family in a ruthless, ultimately grotesque fashion. On the face of it, it's a soap opera, but what makes it extraordinary, aside from the beauty of the prose, is the author's gift for inhabiting every energetic strain of his breathing animal creations. Rex and Margot are absolutely evil, but they are also full of fierce life, wit, and supple, eel-like charm. Nabokov can step inside their cruelty and vitality almost as if it were an electrical current, then step out again and enter the much slower, cooler ambiance of their poor stooge Albinus, or the person of Albinus's bland, taffy-sweet wife, and emerge again, all in a flash. His expanded and detached sensibility can hold them all in a state of dazzling and organic movement, which is a mimicry of life's truth in the deepest sense. The ability to do this requires a great understanding of and regard for life that is, I think, a kind of love.

Sometimes when I write stories, my original impetus is small in the sense that it's personal. I'm perplexed or upset about something, and I need to address or unravel it, so I write about it, literally or metaphorically. It's the same kind of egotistical engine I mentioned earlier; it's got a lot of forward drive. But as I write the story, something happens. The drive is still there, but I lose interest in it because I'm noticing other things, and I'm no longer sure

I want only to go forward. John, in the story about Patty and John, is not a person I would like in real life. But on intuition, I told the story from his point of view. Once I inhabited his body, as he sat on an airplane, "rolling a greasy peanut between two fingers," I could feel how he'd gotten to the point where it seemed right to mistreat Patty. That didn't make it right, but it was impossible not to feel for him — or perhaps simply *feel* him — and thus see the story more deeply.

In another story, a lonely, middle-aged woman who has just learned of the death of an abusive former love goes to a party, gets drunk, and brings home a callow young man. The encounter goes badly, and when morning comes she is alone in bed with her unhappy memories. The situation is desolate, but it's also funny, ugly, tender, mean, affectionate, phony, and genuine all at once. At the very end, she hears her neighbors outside her window discussing the bonnets they're going to wear to the Easter parade. The situation may be bleak, but life is still outside the window, lively and mobile.

What I'm describing is a kind of integration because it requires holding many disparate elements together in a fluid mosaic: the middle-aged woman's self-wounding sexuality is present with her desperation, as well as her humor, her pain, her self-possession, and her compassion. John's brutish dullness is present with his sensitivity, his cowardice, his ineptness, and his strength. When I start writing a story, I don't feel like I'm integrating anything; I feel like I'm marching through mud. But at least some of the time there comes a moment when I feel I'm carrying all the elements I've just described and more in a big, clear bowl. It doesn't feel like I'm containing them. It feels like I'm bringing them into being and letting them be, exactly as they are. My perplexity and upset may still be there, but they are no longer the main event. I feel sadness because much of what is in that bowl is sad. But because of that tender sadness, I also feel humility and joy and love. It's strange because much of what I write about does not seem loving. But to write it makes me feel love.

Rent Retards the Revolution!

DARIUS JAMES
(AKA DR. SNAKESKIN)

WHEN THIS VOLUME'S EDITOR, Will Blythe, first telephoned and asked "Why do you write?" I paused in the middle of the sentence I was composing on my PowerBook, adjusted my Lt. Uhuru headset telephone, and thought for a moment. Finally, I said:

"I write because I can't *paint*."

"Good opening line," he said, encouraging.

"Maybe," I said, dubious — knowing, since "all writing is rewriting," that first sentences are usually trashed.

"There's five hundred bucks in it," he said.

Five hundred dollars would appeal to me only if there was a quick turnaround between the time I delivered the piece and Little, Brown's accounting department sent a check. But that wasn't going to happen, I knew. Publishing houses and record companies take their precious time about paying anybody anything (royalty statements are a great source of amusement for the published author. For example, my last book has a cult following in countries it hasn't even been *published* in [we're talking radio, TV, newspaper, fanzine, and Web-site coverage]. And yet, the last statement I received from my publisher said it earned . . . what? *Twenty-two dollars?*). By the time Time Warner parted with its money, and I actually held it between my fingers, the check would have instantly evaporated in the face of mounting debts. Gone in a puff of smoke. *Poof!* So money wasn't a temptation for this particular exercise.

"And you'll be in the company of writers like Norman Mailer," he added.

Norman Mailer? What had I read by Mailer? "The White Negro"? When was that published? In the fifties? Around the time of *Deer Park*? And it wasn't even one of his "fuggin" novels. It was an essay about how if white people really wanted to be "hip," they had to act like psychotic Negroes. Or some silly shit like that. The only thing I have in common with Mailer is that we're both from Long Branch, New Jersey (in fact, my father claims that when he was a child, he used to sell empty pop bottles to a man he believed was Mailer's dad, suggesting he brewed backyard 'shine). Being seen between the same covers as the Pugnacious Norm was not an enticement for me, either.

Frankly, I was reluctant to take on another assignment. I was under deadline for a long-term commission I had accepted, and I was anxious to return to my novel.

"Y'know," Will began, sensing my reluctance, "I was rereading *That's Blaxploitation!*, and I really thought it was a good book. I mean, there's a lot of really good writing there."

Why did he have to say that? Money and the allure of possible prestige weren't going to corral me into an exercise that would be of no value other than to remind me of the original reasons I do this shit in the first place. But I'm a sucker for flattery. Appeal to my vanity, I'm your friend for life.

"OK, I'll do it," I said, "but I've got this thing to finish first. I should be done by next week."

Will didn't realize that he would not only be acting as editor, but would take on the role of dentist as well, pulling this essay out of me as if he were pulling teeth. The "thing" I had to finish dragged on for another six months.

During those six months, I realized that much of what I write has little to do with why I write. And as I thought more and more about this, I found myself asking, with no small amount of cynicism and disgust, Why *do* I write? And why do I write *now?*

Up until the age of eighteen, I planned to be a painter (or a soldier in the overthrow of the American government, whichever came first — the bullet or the paintbrush). Throughout childhood, I was exposed to the worlds of painting and sculpture by my father, a trained painter/sculptor himself. My father taught me how to see creatively. And taught me what it meant to be a painter.

Painters were iconoclasts, people of defiant and singular vision, who were misunderstood and outcast by society. But it was these same "outcasts," these people who were deemed "insane" by the conventional social order, who created works of precious and substantial beauty. That, my father said, was a meaningful and worthwhile thing to do. So I painted.

But I also wrote. As a child, at age eight, my earliest writings were scripts for the monster movies I shot in a nearby woods with my wind-up 8mm camera. Later, since I also wanted to act, I wrote plays. My more "serious," purposeful writing grew out of the emotional crisis of teenhood. Then, confused by questions concerning identity, drugs, sex, authority, the hypocrisy of the

American mainstream, I wrote because I felt powerless and writing gave me a voice, words allowed me to define the world, they provided me with secure ground to stand on. I wrote to understand my battles, to clarify my thoughts, to make clear who I was, who I was going to be.

I also wrote to understand my rage. Now, looking back, I could attribute it to a number of things, like my mother's early death, or institutional racism; but for the purposes of this essay, I am going to focus on the salient details of one key primal incident.

One night in 1959, when I was four years old, and in the care of a neighbor while my parents were away at work, I rushed out of the apartment, down the stairs, and out into the street. When I turned my head to look back, I was knocked out of my shoes by a speeding car and flung forty feet through the air. The accident left me paralyzed, brain-damaged, and in a coma.

At the hospital, the doctors explained to my parents that there was nothing they could do. I was going to die.

But then my great-aunt Amelia Nixon appeared at my bedside. And in the company of a hougan priest (or "jackleg preacher," as my father called him), she prayed over my small and battered body. I revived after four days.

In my comatose state, I had a tunnel-of-white-light experience. I have vivid recollections of ascending upward through a cloud of fog, draped only in a gown of silver mist. And, quite abruptly, descending back down to earth.

"It wasn't my time to die," I said upon opening my eyes. "So God sent me back." Apparently, once I floated to wherever I was drifting, some weird white place that echoed with deep bass voices singing spooky Negro spirituals, I made a "cross-my-heart-and-hope-to-die"–type promise to whoever was in charge of controlling matters of Life and Death, and was sent back (and given the number of Satanists I count among my friends, I'm sure that's one broken promise I'm gonna pay for BIGTIME!!).

Needless to say, my recovery was a miracle. The doctors were amazed, my parents were grateful, and in spite of the medical prediction that I would be dead by the age of ten, I grew up to be a shiftless, no-account bohemian writer.

But supernatural intervention aside, I was still paralyzed and unable to walk. One night, after weeks in the hospital, frustrated by my bedridden state, I climbed out of my bed, shimmied down its leg, and began to crawl in an attempt to regain my ability to walk.

A nurse found me on the floor. She began screaming at me, calling me names, her face red and distorted with anger (it was a face I would see on teachers, principals, etc., over and over and over again throughout my childhood). The nurse then picked me up, dropped me on the mattress, and trapped me under a mosquito net tied to the bed's four corners.

As I fought against the netting, screaming in stark terror, a blond-haired boy whose head was wrapped in bandages because he had been kicked by a horse sat in my room and *laughed* at me.

The humiliation, confusion, terror, and overall helplessness I experienced in that situation were at the core of the feelings of powerless and voiceless rage I needed to understand and control in teenhood. And it was writing that helped me bring those feelings into perspective. I found power in words. I discovered I could call things into being with words. Writing was my form of magick, in Crowley's fullest sense of the term.

It was while attending the Educational Center for the Arts, a high school devoted to the "creative arts" in New Haven, Connecticut, that I made the decision to switch from painting to writing. I was in drawing class one afternoon, studying the line of a drawing I had done, and I realized that if I had to rely on painting for my livelihood, I was going to starve to death. For reasons that were intuitive instead of logical, I felt I would have a better chance of surviving as a writer. There was no concrete reason for feeling this; it was a vision I accepted on faith. Additionally, I could write without betraying the values and aspirations my father had instilled in me as a child.

More important, I had discovered, through writing, that I was able to transport myself into a wholly consuming imaginative world, one that affected all five senses, and was able to bring back the imagery and raw experience of that state and describe it in vivid and exacting detail. This was something I was unable to achieve through my efforts in painting. I was, however, able to achieve a similar transport as a result of the acting classes I attended in my high school.

Writing, acting, and painting taught me an important lesson: all art is interrelated, and writing is adaptable to a variety of expressive mediums. Writing does not necessarily involve the published word.

As this was the seventies, the other element in all of this was that psychedelic chemical of schizophrenic fun, LSD. I found I could re-create an acid trip I had taken, simulate it in words on paper, and have a reader experience similar sensations. This, actually, is the reason I write: the answer buried inside a platitude reeking with the rancid stench of patchouli oil:

"Revolution begins with a change in consciousness."

My writing is dedicated to fomenting that change. Writing should detonate in your brain like a strong dosage of acid, exploding in an abundance of color, attacking all that is accepted as sacred and true, rearranging, changing all sense and sensibility. Writing should dump the jigsaw puzzle of reality on the ground. Let the reader put the pieces back together again.

None of this answers why I am cynical. Or why I feel disgusted. When I ask myself, Why do I write? the question is superseded by another: What does writing mean to New York publishing?

I grew up influenced by publications like Paul Krassner's *Realist*, *Ramparts*, the *Evergreen Review*, and *Avant Garde*, and publishers like Grove Press under Barney Rosset and Fred Jordan. For me, it was the last really daring period in American publishing. Writers were actually allowed to write then, to write freely and challenge their readership with provocative ideas. That situation really doesn't exist anymore.

Now, once a manuscript leaves a writer's hands for those of a commercial publisher, it becomes a product to be marketed and sold. It means little more than that. And the really sad part is, publishers have proved themselves to be *poor marketers*. How is it that a publisher can spend $150,000 on a writer's advance, and once the book is published, no one ever knows it exists?

Magazines are no better. Intelligent journalism is truncated into demographically dictated copy to justify occupying space purchased by corporate advertisers. It appears to me that severe restrictions have been placed on the published word.

And in the midst of all this, I continually find myself torn between the demands of writing that fulfills my original, acid-inspired intent. And grinding out bullshit for slick, no-brain publications to pay the rent. Rent keeps winning out. *And it's retarding the revolution!*

So why do I continue to write at all? Why do I continue to suffer through the frustration and heartbreak? As the late Michael O'Donoghue once said, "It beats digging ditches!"

The War We Can't Win, We Can't Lose, We Can't Quit

BARRY HANNAH

I ALWAYS EXPERIENCE a mild depression whenever I type up what I have written. This act seems redundant. The work has already been done. I adore the praise of the public, no mistake. But the primary motive must be unpublic. Much more, I'd guess, the inner journey of the imagination itself. There is the ecstasy. The rest is simply good. Some money, a little fame. Not to be rolled over like scuttling claws by the sands of time. Et cetera.

I write out of a greed for lives and language. A need to listen to the orchestra of living. It is often said that a writer is more alive than his peers. But I believe he might also be deader than his peers, a sort of narcoleptic who requires constant waking up by his own imaginative work. He is closer to sleep and dream, and his memory is more haunted, thus more precise.

I write to live, and I write to share. The Original Creator's version seems random and fascistic, but there are enough consistencies, if you wait and watch for them, to give remarkable tales. You must wake up terribly to catch them, even though what you produce may be close to dreams.

My life seems precious, even though often sad, and crammed with mystery. My past seems a fine gray, like good old movie rain. I forget almost nothing. Even when I was a drunk I recalled too much, and hence was forced to relive events in an agony of shame. Friends and confederates are often astounded by what I remember of certain afternoons an age ago — weather, dress, music, mots. A blessing and a curse. I feel superior to nobody because of the gift, and in other talents I rank very low. I do not rate myself highly in thought, for instance. I find life too vivid for thought, really. Thus I go about preaching, of course, that thought is overrated.

I see them pass still, the little old tiny-headed women of Clinton, Mississippi, in the fifties, in their giant cars on the brick streets. Or on their porches or at their azalea beds scolding dogs, then me; nestled in the pews and bobbing heads in the aisles of the church. Bringing in their covered dishes to church suppers. They established the tone of my world. All of them dead or ancient beyond years now. They observed and accounted. I fled them, I was a creature of the night, a little sinner. Or was I only paranoid, like the biblical thief who fleeth when none pursueth? Those days when they were big, these women, in my youth. But now I see their replicates in my grown town, don't I? I always wanted to explain to them how they didn't know how it was, they hadn't the faintest. I picked up the rhythms of scripture for my tales, I'm certain, but it was mystery and sin that had me. I was not the echo for the voices of the tiny-headed women. Was not antiphonal to their voices. I was the dreadful opposite voice to whatever they asserted, the polar howling wretch. In Baptist songs I always liked where you were a wretch or a worm, or just as I am, helpless.

But many of the women were kind, too kind, to me. Mrs. Bunyard in the third grade, why she encouraged my tales and lies, so long as I wrote them down. Even at the same time she made us wash out our mouths with hard soap for swearing, or even for finding any humor in the term *jackass* at all. This was in the good days when teachers listened patiently to your explanations, then beat hell out of you with a holed board. Fiction is work, and I suppose there would be no fiction in the Garden of Eden until the apple and the Fall. Begins the mystery of evil, or of the Other. And the making of books of which there is no end, as warned in Ecclesiastes.

Another kind woman, Mrs. Ashley, was the object of an early mystery, such things as I have been obsessed to declare. I have never written about this, but there was a boy — M., I'll call him — in the Royal Ambassadors with us. He was one of us, I insist. Mrs. Ashley was ward for us boys of the church. One day she took us to the circus in Jackson. M. did not go with us. But while we were away, he attacked Mrs. Ashley's bedroom. Trouble of the brain, a sudden cyclone of it. M. destroyed many items, both costly and worthless. He did not steal. He simply wrecked the place and left it so. There was no explanation. He was not jealous of the circus; he could have gone. But he chose not to. He was a silent, tall boy with wide gray eyes. Nobody recalled his saying much at all, only a mutter or whisper every now and then when he was pressed. Nothing was done to him, but he sank off the

town map. He disappeared into the scandal. I cannot even remember his reappearance, though I know he still came to church
and school. But he was erased from our eyes by his pathology. Nobody wanted to look at him. The fury hidden in M. We looked
away, ashamed for him. Where is he now? What is there to say for
him? What is his story? What is it, M.? Please deliver. No. So I'll
write one for you, pal, these many years from you. It still matters.
And there at the center, kind little tiny-headed Mrs. Ashley, who
loved all her boys. And M., this was the thing. He was one of us,
he was no stranger.

The Furies turned up the volume of our own inner voices, it is
told. Such was their punishment. These voices want both defini-
tion and deliverance. So I write to both record them and free myself of them. Once you are into the life of writing, you are never
really rid of the inner voices, and they are certainly not all your
own. They will exhaust themselves for a time, but then there will
be another siege and you have to sit down and do something
about it.

Even as a Baptist Christian woman, my mother told yarns. She
would be telling about events when I had accompanied her, and
I would know that what she told had not happened. I believe she
was completely unconscious that she was enlarging on the truth.
Otherwise she would know I could shoot her down, as an eyewit-
ness. I think it was the Irish in her. To my father I owe a sense of
diction. I never heard my father make a grammatical error. He
was an insurance salesman and then a banker. His customers
were Jews and blacks as well as the usual whites. People trusted
him. He would not lie, and he never importuned. I don't believe
he had a sales pitch at all. Because of Depression poverty at home,
he had been unable to finish at the university. He loved knowledge and good language all the more for that, and read a book a

day when he retired, a solid and respected success. He told me once about the dog and the robin at a service station in Forest, Mississippi. The dog adopted a wounded robin the owner had in a box under the counter. He licked and nuzzled the robin. The robin was almost well after two weeks and began hopping around the station, not quite able to fly yet. Then the dog, ever faithful to his friend, began playing with it. Unintentionally, he killed the robin. Then the dog was very sad. The men of the station, too, were in black grief. My dad told me this story in a faraway voice full of tenderness and wonder. There was no moral. The whole thing had been both wonderful and terrible. Whatever kindness there is in my work I owe to my parents and to the unflagging love of my brothers and sister, who all told tales and gave me the world. I was spoiled rotten, late babe that I was, and inherited great pieces of their lives before me.

I have evermore been amazed by bursts of kindness in improbable times, the warm hand in dire straits.

But it was an eruption of vileness unprovoked by anything beyond local ennui that marked my first public art, and it was theater. I still remember the complete happiness of making that tape. Reel-to-reel recorders were avant-garde where we lived. Four pals and I set about enacting a wrestling match with commentary, with a few jokes about prominent parochial fools — the Dead Deacon, the Choir Hag, Minister Masturbo, Butt Ream Rob, the Renegade Cheerleader. This was high adolescence, a valedictory to high school, and we had wild fun making it in the instrument room of the band hall. But the tape fell into the principal's hands. He announced over the public address system to the entire student body that something had fallen into his hands, as he put it. It was so corrupt that it had shaken his faith in Youth In Our World. It was a sad, sad artifact, a thing that would crush, just crush the parents of the offenders if they knew. He paused. Was he weeping, or just stringing out the fear? Cold chills took me. This seemed the end, expulsion. But nothing was ever done. Over and over I recalled my contribution to the tape, where the Dead Deacon "was kicked in his giant balls just aflappin' out of his trunks there. . . . He seems to be, oh, no . . . he's vomiting out . . . what . . . waves, I tell you . . . of turnip greens . . . my holy God!" There was no redeeming theme. It was no dreadful sermonette. It was just dreadful. But it was precious, I tell you. It was my art. And it was out there in the hands of the public. Many years later the principal, in his senility, drove down a sidewalk and into a store in a remote town. When I heard this I immediately thought of our tape.

Then to correct the tape, a fantasy, with Upont, I'll call him.

Upont was from St. Louis, and even at eighteen he looked seedy. He had big whiskered cheeks, a slouch, and the waist of a man deep into middle age. He played third-chair trumpet in the marching band, and even his cornet was nasty, green, brown, and splotched, leaking saliva at the spit valve. But he was one of us. He had a nasty wit and a big-city accent we'd hardly heard, so that even the mildest comments from him sounded cynical and decorated with slime. Actually, we thought he was fairly wonderful, and he hung with us in the room, the cafeteria, vespers, there at the college. I guess it was a college. They called it a college. Very Christerly. Conscious of the far mission fields but not of the world.

I was at the local movie house on the big hill, and there was some commotion in the lobby. Small children coming down the stairs to the balcony and pointing upward from where they'd fled. I went up there and in the front balcony seat was Upont with his arm across the shoulders of a small local boy. The boy was frozen there as Upont whispered in his ear and then fastened a tongue on his cheek. The boy just sat staring ahead. This was the thing, just as Upont was the thing. He was one of us, he was Youth In Our World. I cannot forget his utter obliviousness, his helpless tonguing of the child, his whispers. Children around them had fled with little howls of alarm, baffled nausea, signs of throwing up. Upont was heedless, too deep and gone into it. And the boy was allowing it. He seemed fascinated by it all. A first in our time, in our town. It could not be. One of us. It took Mrs. Moddy, one of those tiny-headed women, who ran the movie house, to separate them. I was so wretchedly astonished that I just hung there, mouth open, then quickly fled out the doors and down the hill, lest I be connected to Upont. When I saw my pals in the dorm room I could hardly speak. There seemed to be no straight narration to the event. Grave new world. This was no fantasy, no tape.

Upont was "withdrawn" from the college, as the books have it. We did not much discuss him, but he was still in the room with us. The voices began in my head, and never have I set Upont down in print until now.

The fact is, in a real way, Upont's passion was more sublime, even in its horror, than was our wrestling skit, which was only teenage filth. And the child, this is what kept me going. Just sat there, tongued, whispered to, fascinated. He was ready. You had to gather Upont was a pro. He could spot them. And who could know whether this illicit tenderness might one day proceed to a cyclone of destruction, as with M.'s strange afternoon. Even homicide, I discovered later.

I must get this right.

Must tell it for all of us.

Especially those bright and hungry pals I ran with in school, always my best audience, forever.

It is clear now I had no real stories through college, though I was bragged on by my poet teacher and even accused of plagiarism by another old-bat teacher who wrote verse for greeting cards. My work was bursts of expression that imitated content and charmed others. The fact is, I wanted to write long before I had anything to say. I don't find this condition at all unusual in young writers, good or bad. A sort of attuned restlessness. Often it is simply an overriding need to talk. A sort of transcribed logorrhea, worse than decent gossip. I've taught these people, forever blasting away in high-volume, wretched detail, solidly in love with their own noise. I must say, I was never infatuated by my own voice. It was the ideal inner voices that took me, and they came from everywhere, especially Hemingway, Joyce, Henry Miller, and later Flannery O'Connor. Like many Mississippians, I shied away from Faulkner, who was at once remote and right there in your own backyard, the powerful resident alien. Having read a little of him, I sensed I would be overcome by him, and had a dread, in fact, that he might be the last word. That I would wind up a pining, third-rate echo, like many another Southerner. Then T. S. Eliot, especially "Prufrock." But the earliest great howler who made me want to make the team was the badly forgotten Dylan Thomas, whose voice seemed available everywhere in English departments in the fifties and sixties. It seemed to me a fine thing to get drunk and just start being Welsh and crowing surrealism, as I perceived it. Put that against the sullen bitchery of Holden Caulfield, which charmed almost everybody my age, and you would be cooking. Miles Davis might one day shake your hand. He was God, and that would be very nice.

On a pier in the early sixties, Bay St. Louis, with a fine-looking girl who was dumping me but being pleasant about it, I accidentally declared myself. The brown waves of the two-rivered bay of the Gulf of Mexico were lapping against the piling, and we were alone. Maybe she wanted me to hurt a little, come to think of it. She was in a two-piece red, white, and blue swimsuit, blond hair on her shoulders that broke your heart. She was a smart girl from Millsaps College, but from a poor family in an old gray board house. Her father stamped the price on cans at the grocery. Her mother was frankly mercenary. I was in the running when I was premed, very hot. Then it became known I had changed to English major, and I was cold. Nancy, however, thought this needed a polite farewell, because she did like me. I was in street clothes and she was near nude. But what will you *do?* she asked me. I had no idea. I had no interest in teaching, only in my stories and wretched Beat poems. But I blurted, "Protect the King's English," just to be ironic, hip, careless. I felt like a very mocked knight at the time, a sad punk, really, but what I said is what I have tried to do all these years, even when I had nothing much to say. The language still strikes me as a miracle, a thing the deepest mind adores. At its best, when you lose your arrogance and are least selfish, it can sing back to you almost as a disembodied friend.

I think of those moments in Faulkner, Beckett, and Holy Scripture when the words seem absolutely final, bodiless, disattached, as out of a cloud of huge necessity. My desire is to come even closer to that team — to be that lucky, to be touched by such grace. I do believe that as you write more, and age, the arrogance and most of the vanity go. Or it is a vanity met with vast gratitude, that you were hit by something as you stood in the way of it, that anybody is listening. When you are ashamed and revising your comments to old girlfriends of thirty years ago, you might be shocked to find out you really have nothing much better now than what you said in the first place. This is what I would tell her now: I want to say good stuff.

I finally had a real story at age twenty-three up in Fayetteville, Arkansas.

This followed a near–religious conversion tedious to everybody but me, I'd guess. I'll only say that I became more committed to people who could never tell their own stories and that I was no longer ashamed of being from the most derided state in the union.

Another time I was fishing one Saturday afternoon with my father, my nephews, and my small oldest son, Po, who was afire with Jimi Hendrix at the time. We were catching big bass, all of us up and down the dam, with minnows on cane poles. My father sat there in his lawn chair with his vodka and his cigar, king of the hill. All the nephews, his grandchildren, were rushing to bait his hook as he presided there. I had a novel out after enormous work. It had been celebrated widely, though it sold nothing, and I was a whole man. The sun went behind a cloud and the wind went up, and we were almost dark, in a sudden chilly breeze, a momentary violent change almost as if to another, northern geography. In July, out of the heat, it seemed pure magic, and it felt wonderful. I knelt there consumed by a decision. A huge bass suddenly grabbed my line. I went into a spiritual ecstasy. My family was all around me, we were in heaven. You could cut the joy with a knife. We all felt it, though nobody spoke. This is it, this is it, my life! To say good stuff, like this. To say it, maybe so well they won't forget. This is it. Thanks to God. Later, before his death, my father told me he had never had a better day. He caught a seven-pound bass, the family record. But that's not what I mean, son, he said. The other day my son, out of nowhere, asked me, "Dad, do you remember that day on Elwood Ratliff's dam?"

Twenty years ago I was out in the woods alone. The weather was clear and very cold, but felt good. I had a Pall Mall in my hand and I walked into an old abandoned cabin of the Roosevelt era. Inside the cabin was just a bit warmer than out. A dusty tin bed with a thin mattress on brown springs. I wanted to light the Pall Mall very badly, but I waited awhile for the dark. The hairs of a feral dog lay in a circle on the planks in front of the hearth. In the last grip of faint grays, I lit the cigarette, and the smoke felt exquisitely good inside me. I knew I was pledged to something. This lonesomeness, this cold lost place I would soon warm up. Nobody knew where I was, nobody. It wanted to be lived in here. I knew life would be sad but quite fine then. I felt a hum of joy in my head. Like some old muttering conquistador stumbled up with a flag to ram the staff into God knows what mud.

Forever afterward I would crave abandoned rooms in lost places, me with my pencil and paper. I would mount a small country here. The frame was already there, you were not really a conquistador, let's not kid our girlfriends. But you would warm up and put something in this hole. It might leak a little bit, but it would be yours.

From all my military readings I have gleaned the comment most pertinent to me and the gals and pals desperately given over to the writing life. The writer meant Korea and Vietnam, but he put his truth to the exact same glory and grief of our efforts: "It's the war we can't win, we can't lose, we can't quit."

I'm waiting, however, for the future priest to be kicking around shards of our old cabins. He finds some pages: My God, it's paper, ancient paper. He bends over, holding the cigarette pack–sized computer to his shirt pocket so it won't fall out.

Poor devils, the old scribes, jabber jabber, yadda yadda, he says. But wait, this is pretty good.

Collecting Myself

TOM CHIARELLA

I CAN'T DO MUCH of anything, except write.

I have no jump shot. I can't balance my checkbook. Small machinery puzzles me. I have no nose for news. Cooking bores me. I don't concentrate on physical tasks very well. I can't stack cans, lift weights, or knead bread. I'm lousy with small details. Can't cut a square corner on a true piece of lumber. I don't proofread well. I like cameras, but I take shitty pictures. I enjoy certain paintings but have no heart for museums. Money? Forget it. I'm not good with money.

I'm not particularly strong. Running hurts me, and I'm dreadfully slow. I'm an OK driver, but I doze off after long distances. I fancy myself a dancer, but I've noticed that my partners must be very drunk to enjoy my lead. I'm not photogenic. I'm wildly afraid of heights and don't much like the dark. I have quick hands but no muscle memory. At work, I bungle the routine stuff and bear down to dig myself out of holes when things pile up. I do not sleep well in the summers.

The things I *can* do are embarrassingly useless. I can walk a long way, but I have to talk to myself along the route, telling fantastic lies, carrying on imaginary conversations with long-dead historical figures in which I convince them to make different choices, thus changing history. I must look like a schizophrenic. This embarrasses me. I can drink a lot of liquor, but since my thirtieth birthday, the headaches have become wildly punishing. I have never, to my memory, vomited, but my insides often ache, making it hard to predict from day to day what my mood will be. I have passed a kidney stone and am obsessed with the likelihood that I'll pass another. I am a reasonable cartoonist, but I can't draw the same character twice. I can post-up in basketball, which doesn't help me much since I can't jump. I used to be able to hit a baseball, too, but the skill abandoned me when I needed it most — in the clutch, when-push-came-to-shove, whatever. Suffice it to say, once I could hit a baseball. No more.

That said, I'm fat, overly impressed by wealth, and can remember by name only nine of the thirty-two classes I took in college. I never finished *Moby-Dick*. I can't play casino blackjack — not for long periods of time, anyway, and not when I'm drinking. I'm a reasonable poker player, but I've never played high stakes, so who's to say? Every putt I've ever made in golf has been a matter of pure luck or overwhelming fear, and I play a lot of golf. My penis is on the short side. My grades in school were marginal, and even so I cheated on tests in high school, college, and graduate school. I've never hit another man square or fair, except my brother, and only when he was much smaller than me. Someone else does my taxes. My father buys my stocks. I do mow my own lawn, but it looks better when other people do it. My mother taught me to like gardening, but from year to year my perennials remain clumped and fisted; my annuals never flourish beyond the edges of their pots.

In short, I do a lot, but I don't do it particularly well. Indeed, there is nothing I do well. But I write. I always will. Everything I've done — all that I have survived, the things I've learned, what leaps I have forced upon myself, the choices I've made, the mistakes I've brought upon myself — all of it has come through writing. For me, writing is neither therapy nor solace. It heals no wounds. By itself, it teaches no lessons. It takes me by the nose but leads me nowhere. Still, the only way I get anywhere at all is by writing, so I persist.

Barring the above, I'm not such a terrible loser. Whatever paradoxical glimpses of myself I lend to the world in my everyday life — the loafer, the achiever, the guy with the reasonable touch around the greens, the choke-artist with the putter, the friend, the husband, the father — were all learned by writing. Notice that I did not say by telling stories, I said by writing. Any clown can tell stories. The "storyteller" — that school-visiting, self-aggrandizing, grant-grabbing, tie-to-the-past-claiming performance artist manqué, that scab-picker of the written word who populates the innumerable festivals of art and academe — knows nothing of the chill pleasure of writing. The private blackness. The close-your-eyes-and-render. The inward turn. The improvisation of the storyteller is the shallow end of the creation pool. The storyteller rambles for the village, stumbles forward merely to witness the effect of the tale upon the audience, a loathsome voyeur to himself. The writer is another breed. The writer hoots only to himself, hems without the titter of an audience, employs only the percussion of his heart to keep at it.

It is the most lonely industry. Alone. Crouched. Slouched. Slogging. I write with my own self, no one else. What I love about life — the delicate web of ice in a cocktail glass, the wet roiling soil of spring, the surprising hands of my children — is completely disconnected from the act of writing. You know this stuff: images, fragile, ethereal, distinctly imported from the land of the living. But these things occur to me only when I write. I grab them up. I write to collect the world. Otherwise I stumble through it, nothing more.

About a year ago, I had a car accident. I had been running errands. Allergy shots. Bank deposits. Tire inflations. Prescription refills. At one point I bought two boxes of wine and some beer and set them in the front seat of my Honda. I drove off to drop them at my friend's house for a party we were having later that night. Upon arriving at his house, I realized I had forgotten the ice.

As I was heading back to town, a kid in a hepped-up Mustang plowed into me from the left. All I can remember now — the plume of smoke, the serpentine slice of his tires against the blacktop, my sad little cry of fear ("Not that!") at the moment of impact — is mere snatches. As I write about it, it occurs to me that the impact was thick and juicy, about what it would feel like to hit a cow as hard as you could with a wooden baseball bat, both cruel and unusual. Still, the savage movement of my little car, which spun 540 degrees, struck me as strangely pleasurable. Afterward, the fact of my own survival made me giddy.

But the impact threw my legs across the front seat, into one of the boxes, shattering most of the wine bottles and drenching me in midrange Chardonnay. Thus, pulled from my car, I had a story to tell. Right away. People pressed me for details. Soon the cops were there, wanting to know everything. Why wouldn't they? I was a state trooper's wet dream. I smelled like wine, I couldn't keep my balance, and I'd just been involved in a high-speed collision.

I told them what I could, which was very little. Nothing came together. I knew my name. I knew where the stop sign was and had a clear sense of the mechanics of the collision. Point-A-to-point-B stuff. I relayed what I could. Even then, pinpricked by glass shards, bleary and whiplashed, I was thinking what I always think, not just in moments like this, but in every moment, on every day: I'll survive. I'll write about this. Then I'll know what's happened to me.

This is my first shot at it. It is probably not wise, as there are lawsuits in the offing, depositions still to be made; in situations like this they tell you not to say anything, not to put anything in writing. But really, what else can I do?

Ask a transvestite, "Why are you a transvestite?" and he'll tell you, "Because I wear women's clothes." At least a smart one will. Take his word for it, too. Other transvestites you ask will giggle or take a swipe at you, justify or shrug. Ignore them. They're not talking about themselves. They're responding to you and your reaction to them. The first one, the smart one, is talking about himself, about what he does and why.

I write. The longer I live, the more convinced I become that I cultivate my truest self in this one way. I pay more attention when I'm writing, and I hear myself most clearly when I'm writing. Don't get me wrong: I love to talk. Haggling about a file cabinet at the office, gassing on about the Redskins or spinning ice in my glass while recounting a movie plot, I can jabber with the best of them. But it just ain't me. Not all of me, anyway. The clearest me, the only version of me that I hear, is the one that's writing. If I'm not doing it now, I should be. Otherwise I'm just picking up more crap, starting up something I'll never finish, buying something I don't need, or reading something I couldn't give a shit about. So I write. There's nothing else for me.

Why She Writes

JAYNE ANNE PHILLIPS

The Short Answer

I DON'T KNOW WHY, and I hope I never find out.

Guild Membership, or Working the Hole

I admit I'm given to magical thinking (as though thinking should be anything else), and I would never actually demand of myself an answer to the question. What do I know about myself? Enough to know very little. I wouldn't claim, as a celebrated writer once did, that "whatever is good about me is in the writing, all the rest is shit." The same writer was asked if he had any friends or intimates who weren't writers. "Why would I want to?" he responded — a response I understand and quietly applaud. I think of literary writers as members of a guild of outcasts, a species, through time, of the gifted handicapped, regardless of their success. You see, there really *is* no success — in terms of the writer, as opposed to the work. For the writer, the work is never what you thought it would be, or what you hoped. Sometimes it's better; if the writing is any good, it struggles free of you, and the feeling of being inside it just as it moves away is so brief; a sensual visitation, the brush of His hand. You, on the other hand, are never free, or off the hook, it is never done, writing is a process, book to book, finished piece to abandoned fragment, dream to compulsion, every failure linked to its luminous twin star. Ah, the hook with its gleaming prong, the abyss with its deep, narrow slit, its dark that plummets forever! There is the divided consciousness, the sense of leading a double life, depending on how "normal" the writer appears to be, or tries to appear to be. People have said to me, "You wrote that? You look too normal." You should look *different*, is the implication, you should have four arms or glow in the dark, so we can tell you from the rest of us at a glance and not be fooled. Writers drive cars, hold jobs off and on, raise children, climb mountains, and take out the garbage, but very few have retirement plans. Retirement from what? Thinking? Being? We try to handle our habit (William Burroughs: "I was working the hole with the sailor and we did not do bad"). We go off the rails and lose the job or screw up our relationships, then we pull it together, patch it up, but all the time, while we apologize, castigate ourselves, resolve to do better, the process of writing goes on, the secret reserve is honed and moving, moving toward writing, into writing, until death cancels all.

DOUBLE LIFE, THEN AND NOW

Maybe back then, the expatriates in the cafés of Paris, Jack Kerouac when he was off with the boys instead of living with his mother, Colette with her diaries and lovers, Katherine Anne bedecked in emeralds, maybe they were writers all the time, every minute, the interior life *was* the life. That's like the writer turned inside out, for all the world to see — not a pretty prospect, and not so brave, finally. Much harder to wear the white dress and smuggle notes through the hedge, live on the slim word delivered through the mails from a like mind, drive the carpool, and much riskier, too, because writing might vanish altogether. Writing, never truly fastened up by props, always threatens to flicker out, like the one flame that keeps you breathing, guttered in the draft. Yet writing will not desist. There is no question of stopping. You can be like Rimbaud and stop actually writing the words, but you can't stop wanting to write, needing to; you can't stop leaning toward language. And frankly, if you do stop, nothing will mean anything ever again, and you'll watch all you love, everything you've ever wanted to save, all you need to invent, do a long, slow fade. You must try: commit to the magical, the invisible, while life itself keeps going, doing one thing while you save yourself for another — the writing. So you stand there with one foot in the pit, in the black hole that sucks its own energy into an alternate dimension. Light is inside it, far inside, blinding light. The light starts as glimmer, like phosphorescence on a fly's wings, and bent color, like the bronzy reflections in an oily puddle, and gets brighter, bigger, hotter. You zip on the asbestos suit, deep inside the black slit, and walk through flames. It's not about personality or strength or weakness; the writer may require a cork-lined room, fall down drunk daily, or be a perfectly lovely person. It's about writing. The instant the protection of language falls away, there is the odor of singed hair. Fall back! Fall back! And begin a renewed approach. We're in control of our rituals. We're in control of a repetition of discipline, of sitting in the chair. When something works, it may feel like the strike of lightning or a solar storm, but it's never a sustained climate. The writer can't make it happen, or make it happen again. Deep into a poem, a story, a novel, through practice and the honing of instinct, the writer can begin to follow the work, descend with it, a brain in a diving bell, breathing through a tube.

Open Veins

Despite membership in the guild of outcasts, writers do, by quirk of fate or sex or addiction or parenthood, become intimate with *others*, with those who don't originate from the planet of words and language. *Other* things do happen, but we don't know what they are until we write about them, or think about them in words, or remember them in phrases. Experience, more real than words, vanishes. Intimacy is transitory, but its effect lasts as long as consciousness regards it. Words float memory, awaken desire; words do pull people in, even demanding, haunting words, because language is, finally, a matter of survival. *Mama. I want. Yes. No. Stop. Go.* And more. Human beings can't live without the illusion of meaning, the apprehension of confluence, the endless debate concerning the fault in the stars or in ourselves. The writer is just the messenger, the moving target. People love turning their backs on writers, as they will, repeatedly, turn their backs on themselves. Inside culture, the writer is the talking self. Through history, the writing that lasts is the whisper of conscience, and history regards individual voices in various ways at various times according to the dictates of fashion, whimsy, values, politics. The guild of outcasts is essentially a medieval guild existing in a continual Dark Age, shaman/monks, witch/nuns, working in isolation, playing with fire. When the first illuminated manuscripts were created, few people could read. Now that people are bombarded with image and information and the World Wide Web is an open vein, few people can read. Reading with sustained attention, reading for understanding, reading to cut through random meaninglessness — such reading becomes a subversive act. We're not talking detective books, romance, cookbooks, or self-help. We're talking about the books writers read to feel themselves among allies, to feed themselves, to reach across time and distance, to hope.

NATURE AND NURTURE

The writer is, first, genetically predisposed to write, and second, born into a constellation that nurtures her. That constellation is composed of fixed stars that move through time in concert with one another: the mother, the father, the brothers, the sisters, whoever comprises one's primal family, one's first universe. Whether present or absent, the father and mother first function as magnetic poles, polar opposites, counterparts, North Star, the tip of the Southern Cross. That universe is characterized by relationship and history: the unresolved childhood dilemmas of the mother and father, the passion and/or lonely distance between them, the dashed expectations that may find new life in relationship to the child of the union, the child who takes the place of the counterpart, the child who becomes the parent, the child who becomes the confidant, the child who becomes . . . there are endless variations. But the child who evolves into a writer is the child in the process of becoming, who moves into position, who receives the bad and the good, who notices, who listens, who remembers, who saves, and he or she first does so for the sake of the loved one, the giant who shines such light and casts such shadow. Recognition is burden and blessing: the child is recognized as special, presented with truths or secrets, told stories. Promises are spoken or simply evolve. The writer is not the child who is ignored, or the one simply indulged. More often, the writer is one to whom much is given or entrusted, verbally or spiritually, the one of whom much is expected, the one with whom a bond beyond death is forged. The child is amply influenced, chameleon-like, perhaps, able to leap points of view in a single bound, possessed of a permeable identity. The die is cast. If the child survives, is educated, encounters teachers in books and schools, in streets, on corners, he or she begins to write, becomes an outlaw early on. The giant who first embraced the child may stand back aghast. The writer's first affinity is not to a loyalty, a tradition, a morality, a religion, but to life itself, and to its representation in language. Nothing is taboo. The writer will go anywhere, say anything to get it said; in fact, the writer is bent on doing so. The writer is bent.

TORTURED AND TANTALIZED

Ego enters in, but writing is far too hard and solitary to be sustained by ego. The writer is compelled to write. The writer writes for love: for lost love, perhaps. The writer lives in spiritual debt to the someone or something who needed saving, who first passed on the talisman — language, the gold key in the palm of meaning. Writers of literature don't write for gain or attention or praise, though they'll take all that when they can get it. There are exceptions, but even "successful" writers, when their incomes are averaged out over a working lifetime, do well to make a postman's salary, without the benefits. There are teaching salaries, but teaching shoots writing in the head. Sometimes the writer lives on afterward, blinking to say what he wants. But it's like when you stop smoking: the writer quits teaching, and the lungs pick up in ten weeks, the brain relearns its functions. The writer is an autonomic nervous system, a heart that won't stop pumping. The writer dreams selectively, more attentive to the conversation going on behind him than to the one in which he is engaged. The writer is probably ADD; she values her deficits and often leads with them. The writer is a good mom; he feeds the baby and then forgets where he left it. She's a stalwart soldier; her weapon is in good repair, but she keeps mixing up borders, crossing into occupied territory. They both cook for the troops. They take in strays, recognize wandering souls. Good Buddhists, they ring the bell when it's time to sit. Their practice involves silence, focus, white space, waiting. Alone yet postcoital, associatively drenched, they arrange small, two-dimensional symbols in endless combinations. The avatar is inside the word; there will be an audience soon. Awake, asleep, in every moment of being, the writer stands at the gate. The gate may open. The gate may not. Regardless, the writer can see straight through it.

In Silence

ROBERT STONE

WHEN I BEGAN TO THINK UP stories, as a child, it was because stories were my greatest childhood pleasure. I also found
that in an environment where it was very difficult to gain approval, I could get some positive reinforcement from storytelling.

My interior world felt like confusion, a source of fears and un-
requited aspirations and disappointment. But it was also, as far as
I could determine, where joy originated, and hope for and fantasies of a different, better life.

I made a few discoveries in the earliest stages of my reading that
I never quite got over. One was that a story could be knit together
in such a way that it completely dominated the mind's eye and ear
and became an alternative reality. Certain books and tales
seemed to accomplish this more effectively than others. It was like
the difference between a good trick and an indifferent one.

I also found that a story did not have to end happily to be satisfying. That even stories that made you feel like crying, or did make you cry, like Andersen's or Wilde's fairy tales, provided a certain comfort. They were almost scary to read, because you knew that they would end in your tears. Yet the satisfaction, paradoxical but undeniable, was as intense as that to be had from any funny story. After a while I realized that their secret lay in the fact that they made the world less lonely. Almost every way one felt, it seemed, could be made into a story. About then it occurred to me that stories were about recognizing the way things were. In other words, they were about truth, and truth was important.

Very early on, I thought that the ability to combine character and incident with a measure of that truth was a very fine thing to be able to do. When I was a child, there was a children's card game called Authors that featured writers like Whittier and Dickens, Longfellow and Poe. Although I can't now recall any of the rules of the game, I remember thinking that these characters with their chin-whiskers and feather pens must be great men indeed. (We believed in Great Men then.) There were, as I remember, no women writers in the game, which seems almost impossible now. But I never doubted the stature of these old-fashioned gents. I had a certain sense of what they had done for a living, and I had even read some of their work.

Whittier's "Snowbound" was, I think, the first and most vivid poem I can remember, my first favorite. Like most people, I remember poetry first.

> The sun that brief December day
> Rose cheerless over hills of gray
> And, darkly circled, gave at noon
> A sadder light than waning moon.

And "The Rime of the Ancient Mariner," which I read before I could comprehend its argument but the lines of which haunted me:

> Like one, that one a lonesome road
> Doth walk in fear and dread,
> And having once turned round walks on,
> And turns no more his head;
> Because he knows, a frightful fiend
> Doth close behind him tread.

That got to me.

I thought writing was a great thing to do, and I wanted to do it, too. I was unhandy and unartistic. I could not draw anything but stick figures, or fashion base materials into the shape of something greater. But I loved language; I loved its tricks and rhythms and ironies. Although I had been taught there was a time to keep silence, I thought there were times when the world, in its loneliness, required something other than the vast silence in which we labored. I knew no other way of not being alone in the world than through language.

Eventually the silence came to seem to me like an absence of something that must somehow be invoked. I knew only writing, that message in a bottle, with its artificial sounds and mimicked speech and tropes, as a means of invocation. I knew only narrative as a way of making sense of causality. Silence could be an enemy, a condition to which we had been consigned and to which we must respond. Because I respected the silence, however cold and alien and hostile, I wanted to make that with which I tried to answer it worthy of its terrible majesty.

Who Is That Man Tied to the Mast?

MARK RICHARD

SAY YOU HAVE A "special child," which in the South means one between Down's and dyslexia. Birth him with his father away on army maneuvers along East Texas bayous. Give him his only visitor in the military hospital his father's father, a sometime railroad man, sometime hired gun for Huey Long, with a Louisiana Special Police badge. Take the infant to Manhattan, Kansas, in winter, where the only visitor is a Chinese peeping tom, little yellow face in the windows during the cold nights. Further frighten the mother, aged twenty, with the child's convulsions. There's something "different" about this child, the doctors say.

Move the family to Kirbyville, Texas, where the father cruises timber in the big woods. Fill the back porch with things the father brings home: raccoons, lost bird dogs, stacks of saws and machetes. Give the child a sandbox to play in in which scorpions build nests. Let the mother cut the grass and run over rattlesnakes, shredding them all over the yard. Make the mother cry and miss her mother. Isolate her from the neighbors because she is poor and Catholic. For a playmate, give the child a mongoloid girl who adores him. She is the society doctor's child and is scared of thunder. When it storms, she hides, and only the special child can find her. The doctor's wife comes to the house in desperation. Please help me find my daughter. Here she is, in the culvert, behind a bookcase, in a neighbor's paper tepee. Please come to a party, the doctor's wife sniffs, hugging her daughter. At the party, it goes well for the nervous mother and the forester father until their son bites the arm of a guest and the guest goes to the hospital for stitches and a tetanus shot. The special child can give no reason why. Further isolate the family in the community.

Move the family to a tobacco county in southside Virginia. It is the early sixties, and black families still get around on mule and wagon. Corn grows up the backs of houses, even in town. Crosses burn in yards of black families and Catholics. Crew-cut the special child's hair in the barber shop where all the talk is of niggers and nigger lovers. Give the child the responsibility of another playmate, the neighbor two houses down, Dr. Jim. When Dr. Jim was the child's age, Lee left his army at Appomattox. When Dr. Jim falls down between the corn rows he is always hoeing, the child must run for help. Sometimes the child just squats beside Dr. Jim sprawled in the corn and listens to Dr. Jim talking to the sun. Sometimes in the orange and gray dusk when the world is empty the child lies in the cold backyard grass and watches thousands of starlings swarm Dr. Jim's chimneys. At age five he feels like he is dying in a gloomy world.

Downstairs in the house the family shares is a rough redneck, a good man who brought a war bride home from Italy. The war bride thought the man was American royalty because his name was Prince. Prince is just the man's name. The Italian war bride is beautiful and has borne two daughters; the younger is the special child's age. The elder is a teenager who will soon die of a blood disease. The beautiful Italian wife and the special child's mother smoke Salems and drink Pepsi and cry together on the back steps. They both miss their mothers. In the evening Prince comes home from selling Pontiacs and the forester father comes home from the forest and they drink beer together and wonder about their wives. They take turns mowing the grass around the house.

The company the father works for is clearing the land of trees. The father finds himself clearing the forests off the old battlefields from the Civil War. The earthworks are still there, stuff is still just lying around. He comes home with his pockets full of minnie balls. He buys a mine detector from an army surplus store and the family spends weekends way, way out in the woods. One whole Sunday the father and the mother spend the day digging and digging, finally unearthing a cannon-sized piece of iron agate. The mother stays home after that. On Sunday nights she calls her mother in Louisiana and begs to come home. No, her mother says. You stay. She says all this in Cajun French.

The little girl downstairs is named Debbie. The special child and Debbie play under the big tree where the corn crowds the yard. One day the special child makes nooses and hangs all Debbie's dolls from the tree. Debbie runs crying inside. Estelle, the big black maid, shouts from the back door at the special child to cut the baby dolls down, but she doesn't come out in the yard to make him do this, and he does not. She is frightened of the special child, and he knows this. If he concentrates hard enough, he can make it rain knives on people's heads.

Maybe it would be best if something is done with the special child. The mother and father send him to kindergarten across town where the good folk live. The father has saved his money and has bought a lot to build a house there, across from the General Electric Appliance dealer. Because he spent all his money on the lot, the father has to clear the land himself. He borrows a bulldozer from the timber company and "borrows" some dynamite. One Saturday he accidentally sets the bulldozer on fire. One Sunday he uses too much dynamite to clear a stump and cracks the foundation of the General Electric Appliance dealer. The father decides not to build in that neighborhood after all.

In the kindergarten in that part of town, the special child feels like he is on to something. There are records the teacher he calls Miss Perk lets him play over and over. When the other kids lie on rugs for their naps, she lets him look at her books. During reading hour he sits so close to her that she has to wrap him in her arms while she holds the book. The best stories are the ones Miss Perk tells the class herself. About the little girl whose family was murdered on a boat and the criminal tried to sink the boat. The little girl saw water coming in the portholes, but she thought the criminals were just mopping the decks and doing a sloppy job. Miss Perk tells about the car wreck she saw that was so bloody she dropped a pen on the floor of her car for her son to fetch so he wouldn't have to see the man with the top of his head ripped off like he had been scalped. On Fridays is show and tell, and the special child always brings the same thing in for show and tell: his cat, Mr. Priss. Mr. Priss is a huge, mean tomcat that kills other cats and only lets the special child near him. The special child dresses Mr. Priss in Debbie's baby-doll clothes, especially a yellow raincoat and yellow sou'wester-style rain hat. Then the special child carries Mr. Priss around for hours in a small suitcase. When the mother asks if he has the cat in the suitcase again, the special child always says No mam.

Miss Perk says the way the other children follow the special child around, that the special child will be something someday, but she doesn't say what.

The father and the mother meet some new people. There is a new barber and his wife. The new barber plays the guitar in the kitchen and sings Smoke smoke smoke that cigarette. He is handsome and wears so much oil in his hair that it stains the sofa when he throws back his head to laugh. He likes to laugh a lot. His wife teaches the mother how to dance, how to do the twist. There is another new couple in town, a local boy, sort of a black sheep, from country folk, who went to Asia to be a flight surgeon and is back with his second or third wife, nobody knows for sure. At the reckless doctor's apartment, they drink beer and do the twist and listen to Smothers Brothers albums. They burn candles stuck in Chianti bottles. The special child is always along because there is no money for a baby-sitter, and Estelle will not baby-sit the special child. One night the special child pulls down a book off the doctor's shelf and begins to slowly read aloud from it. The party stops. It is a college book about chemicals. In two months the child will start first grade.

At first, first grade is empty. Most of the children are bringing in the tobacco harvest. The ones who show up are mostly barefoot and dirty, and sleep with their heads on the desks all day. A lot of them have fleas and head lice. Most of them have been up all night tying tobacco sticks.

At first, first grade is incomprehensible to the special child. Of course that is the alphabet, what do you want me to do with it? What do you want me to say about it? What do you want from me? The child wants to get to the books, but the books are for later, the

teacher tells him. You must learn the alphabet first. But the child
has learned all that already: Miss Perk taught him the letters
perched in her lap at her desk while the other children napped,
and he taught himself how they fit together to make words sitting
close to her as she read from children's books and *Life* magazine.
The special child thought the tobacco children had the right idea,
so he put his head on his desk and slept through the A's and B's
and C's.

He won't learn, he doesn't learn, he can't learn, the teachers
tell the mother. He talks back to his teachers, tries to correct their
speech. He was rude to kind Mr. Clary when he came to show the
class some magic tricks. You better get him tested. He might be retarded. And he runs funny.

The special child is supposed to be playing at the General Electric Appliance dealer's house with his son David. The son has a
tube you blow into and a Mercury capsule shoots up in the air and
floats down on a plastic parachute. The special child may have to
steal it, but first he decides to go to visit Miss Perk's. Maybe she
has a book or something. Miss Perk does not disappoint. She is
glad to see the special child. She tells him that the Russians send
men up in Mercury-capsule things and don't let them come back
down. She says if you tune your radio in just right you can hear
their heartbeats stop. She says if you ever see a red light in the
night sky, it's a dead Russian circling the earth forever. Can I
come back and be in your school, Miss Perk? No, you're too big
now. Go home.

Back at the General Electric Appliance house, there's nobody
home. It is too far to walk home, so the child lies in the cold grass
and watches the gray and orange dusk. At dark, his life will be
over. There's a gunshot off in the clay field a ways away, and something like a rocket-fast bumblebee whizzes through the air and

thuds into the ground beside the special child. He stays real still. There's not another one. The child is beginning to learn that things can happen to you that would upset the world if you told about them. He doesn't tell anyone about the thing that buzzed and thumped into the ground by his head.

Y'all should do something with that child, people say. The mother takes the child to Cub Scouts. For the talent show, the mother makes a wig out of brown yarn, and the special child memorizes John F. Kennedy's inaugural speech. They laugh at the child in the wig at the show until he begins his speech. Afterward, there's a lecture on drinking water from the back of the toilet after an atom bomb lands on your town, and everybody practices crawling under tables. For weeks afterward, people stop the child and ask him to do the Kennedy thing, until finally somebody shoots Kennedy in Texas and the child doesn't have to perform at beer parties and on the sidewalk in front of the grocery store anymore.

The mother starts crying watching the Kennedy funeral on the big TV the father bought to lift her spirits. She doesn't stop. The mother won't get out of bed except to cry while she makes little clothes on her sewing machine. She keeps losing babies, and her mother still won't let her come home. The father sends for the mother's sister. They pack a Thanksgiving lunch and drive to Appomattox to look at the battlefields. It rains and then snows and they eat turkey and drink wine in the battlefield parking lot. The mother is happy, and the father buys the special child a Confederate hat. After the sister leaves, the mother loses another baby. The father brings the special child another beagle puppy home. The first one, Mud Puddle, ran away in Texas after the father drove it from Lake Charles, Louisiana, to Kirbyville, Texas, strapped to the roof of the car. He had sedated it, he tried to convince people who were nosy along the way. When they got to Texas, there were bugs stuck all in its front teeth like a car grille. When the dog woke completely up, it ran away.

This dog, in Virginia, the special child calls Hamburger. The mother cries when she sees it in the paper sack. Maybe we need to meet some more friends, the father tells the mother. OK, the mother says, and wipes her eyes. She always does what her husband tells her to do.

There's the big German Gunther with the thick accent and his wife, who manage the dairy on the edge of town. They have a German shepherd named Blitz who does whatever Gunther tells it to do. The special child is frightened of the vats of molasses Gunther uses to feed the cows. The child is more interested in the caricatures down in the cellar of Gunther's old house. Gunther's old house was a speakeasy, and someone drew colorful portraits of the clandestine drinkers on the plaster wall behind the bar. They look like people in town, says the special child. It's probably because the cartoons are the fathers of people in town, says his father.

Gunther's wife finds the special child lying in the cold grass of a pasture watching the sun dissolve in the orange and gray dusk. You shouldn't do that, she tells him. If an ant crawls in your ear, it'll build a nest and your brain will be like an ant farm and it'll make you go insane.

Later on, Gunther falls into a silage bin, and his body is shredded into pieces the size a cow could chew as cud.

The timber company gives the father a partner so they can re-seed the thousands of acres of forests they are clear-cutting down to nothing. Another German. The German knows everything, just ask him, the father says. The German and his wife have two children the special child is supposed to play with. Freddie is the boy's name. Once, when the special child is spending the night, a hurricane comes and Freddie wets the bed and blames it on the special child. After that, the special child breaks a lot of expensive wind-up cars and trains from the Old Country.

From the helicopter the father uses to reseed the forests farther south, you can still see Sherman's march to the sea, the old burnage in new-growth trees, the bright cities that have sprung from the towns the drunken Federal troops torched. Yah, yah, dat iz in der past, says the German, you must let it go.

The father and the German are in North Carolina cutting timber in the bottom of a lake. The dam to make the lake isn't finished yet. The father and the German have become good friends. Sometimes they do their work way back in the deep country away from company supervisors and sometimes they walk through empty old houses on land their company has bought for timber rights. In the attics they find rare books, old stamps, Confederate money. One day eating lunch in the bottom of the lake, the father and the German figure how much more timber has to be cut before the water will reach the shore. They say, You know, if you were able to figure exactly where the shoreline will be, and buy that land, you could make a small fortune.

On the weekends, the father and the German break their promise to take their families to Indian caves they have found and have picnics and ride everybody around on the bush motorcycles they use to put out forest fires. Instead, they spend every extra hour of daylight cutting sight lines with machetes, dragging borrowed surveying equipment and measuring chains around the edge of the empty lake.

The money they give the old black sharecropper for the secret shoreline is all the money they can scrape out of their savings and their banks. The old black sharecropper accepts the first offer the father and the German make on the land left to him by his daddy.

Most of the shoreline property they buy from the timber company, but they need an access road through the old black sharecropper's front yard, past his shack. Everyone knows the lake is coming, but the father and the German don't tell the black sharecropper the size of their shoreline purchase, just as he doesn't tell them he has also eyeballed where the shoreline will appear and is going to use their money to build the state's first black marina, with jukeboxes and barbecue pits, right next to their subdivision. He doesn't tell them they just gave him the seed money to build Huff's Marina and Playland.

Twenty acres of waterfront property, two points with a long, clay, slippery cove between them when the dam closes and the lake floods. The German gets his choice of which half of the property is his because he was somehow able to put up 10 percent more money at the last minute. He chooses the largest point, the one with sandy beaches all around it. The father gets the wet, slippery claybank and muddy point. The father tells the mother it is time to meet some new friends.

Meet the American Oil dealer, the one with the pretty wife from Coinjock, North Carolina, a wide grin, and a Big Daddy next door. Down in the basement of his brand-new brick home, on a brick mantel, the oil dealer has a little ship he put together in college. Most people, if they are even guessing, foot up near the fire, glass-leaning with bourbon, take the little model to be a Viking ship. It is not a Viking ship, even though the little fur-tunicked men seated at both rails pull oars beneath a colorful sail. Who is that man tied to the mast? asks the special child. Upstairs the adults play Monopoly in the kitchen and drink beer until the father drinks a lot of beer and begins to complain about Sherman's march, and Germans, and it is time to go home.

Later on, the special child is guarding his house with his Confederate hat and wooden musket while his mother and father are at the hospital having a baby. The oil dealer drives over in his big car and spends the afternoon with the special child. He has a paper sack full of Japanese soldiers you shoot into the air with a slingshot and they parachute into the shrubbery. He shows the special child how to make a throw-down bomb with matchheads and two bolts, but best of all, in a shoebox he has brought the special child the little ship off the brick mantel and he tells him who Ulysses was. It is a good story. The only part of the story the child does not quite believe is that somehow Ulysses was older than Jesus. He doesn't say anything to the oil dealer because the oil dealer is being nice, but he will have to ask Miss Perk about this later.

Here's some pieces that have come off the ship over the years, the oil dealer says. There are a couple of Ulysses' men in his shirt pocket. Thank you, says the child. The child spends the weekend at the oil dealer's house with his wife and children waiting for his mother and father to come home from the hospital empty-handed again.

More bad luck. The people at the dam the father calls the idiots keep turning the knobs on the water back and forth. One day the father and the German take their families on a surprise picnic to look at their waterfront property, and from a hill above their land they can see the lake, way down there over miles of mud. Then one day they come back and find Mr. Huff sitting on the front porch of his sharecropper's shack surrounded by water. All y'all's land under water, says Mr. Huff. Ain't nothing you can do about it. Man came round and said so. Said it's in your deed. The father and the German go to see a lawyer. Mr. Huff is right.

One night while his mother is fixing supper, bad luck starts for the special child. He is in the living room, where he saw an angel pass through on Easter morning, watching the Three Stooges with the sound turned down real low because the Three Stooges upsets her. It is a good Three Stooges. It is the one where Moe and them run back and forth up and down some train cars and stuff happens and there's a lion loose out of the baggage car, but the best part is when Moe keeps stubbing his toe on somebody's little suitcase every time he runs past it until finally Moe opens the train door and throws the little suitcase off the train into the night, and Moe just doesn't stop there, he keeps throwing suitcases off the train, all by himself, he just keeps throwing people's suitcases off the train in the middle of the night until he looks around and sees that he has thrown everything off the train he possibly could, and then he can relax and be himself again and not be angry. The child has seen this Three Stooges before, but this is his favorite. The only problem this night watching it with the sound turned down real low while his mother cooks supper waiting for the father to come home, the only problem is that partway through the show, the child hears a truck just outside slam on its brakes and blow its horn and he hears a dog yelp and he hears cars slow down and people getting out and men talking and somebody going around the neighborhood knocking on doors and asking Whose dog is that and he hears the people downstairs answer the door, he hears Prince say Yeah, he thinks he knows whose dog it is, and he hears Prince call up the staircase to the mother she might want to come down 'cause it looks like a dog looking like their dog got hit by a log truck, and the mother says Oh no, and comes in where the child is watching Moe start to throw the suitcases from the train with the sound turned down real low, and she says We'd better go see about Hamburger, but the child does not move from the TV he is kneeling so close in front of, and the mother has her coat on now and says Did you hear me? Hamburger just got hit by a truck and still the child does not move, does not make movements to get up even though he loves his dog and if it is true that his dog is dead then he will want to die as well, but the child kneels in front of the TV and concentrates on Moe throwing the suitcases off the train, because deep inside him he knows that he can concentrate really hard, like when he learned the Kennedy speech, like when he stepped on a copperhead and the snake would not bite him even though it should have, the child knows that if he can only concentrate hard enough that Moe will keep throwing everything off the train forever and time will stand still and he will never have to die because he will not have to go downstairs and see his dog twisted and smeared across the street and hear somebody, maybe the nervous log-truck driver, maybe Prince himself, make a joke about what his dog's name used to be and what the dog is now.

He never goes downstairs, even though he concentrates in his mind to make the story continue forever and the news comes on and his mother appears up from the street and looks at him in a new way like maybe what some people and teachers say about him is true and maybe they ought to have him tested.

The father comes home late that evening after hand-digging a firebreak almost by himself down in some cornpone county where the rednecks came out to watch the fire burn a stand of company pine. For about eighteen hours the father and a pulp-wood contractor and his pimply son worked to turn a fire that sometimes stood fifty feet high in the trees over their heads and flanked them a hundred yards on either side, sometimes closing. It was good not having to think about his life savings underwater or his sad wife and her lost babies or his strange son or Sherman's march, digging, shoveling, trying to breathe. The father can barely climb the steps up to the top of their house. All he wants is a drink and a hot soak. He has recently started sipping whiskey rather than the beer. His hands are raw and his back and shoulders ache. In the last hours the fire lit a turpentine stump and about a hundred snakes spat themselves up out of the ground and flowed like a stream over his boots. His nerves are still a little jangly.

Up at the top of the stairs stands his special child hardly able to catch his breath from crying so hard and not wanting to wake his mother. The special child clings to his pants legs by the pockets and tells him he wants to die because his dog Hamburger is dead, isn't there something his daddy can do about it, and all the father can do about it is pet the boy's head and go back downstairs, get the fire shovel out of the back of his truck, and hope he has enough strength to bury what is left of the little dog in the corner of the cornfield out back of the house.

Here is some more luck the German and the father have. One day they are driving the German's Volkswagen bus up a cliff road to check on some land the company is clearing. A log truck loaded with company logs comes around a corner in the middle of the road. The German also always drives in the middle of the road. In the collision the flat-fronted bus folds forward and the German's legs are pinned and broken in several places. The father is luckier. He raises his arms to his face in time to protect it as he goes through the windshield. In his luck, he flies through the windshield, and then over the cliff. He goes over the cliff and lands on some railroad tracks at the bottom. Luckily, the train is late that day. They find his eyeglasses perfectly balanced on a train rail, unbroken.

Here are some of the people who comfort the family: Dr. Jim's wife on the one side of the house. The other next-door neighbors, the Shorts, and next to them, the Longs. The special child has always thought it would be nice to live between them. Down the street a whole block of Misses — Miss Laura, Miss Effie, Miss Robert, and Miss Henrietta, who used to be a Mrs. until her husband had a heart attack and died the first time they had sex, everyone said. Down the next block, another, older block of spinsters, bitter children of the Reconstruction too old to come out to bring food but send Negro maids with bags of bad fruit from trees in their yards. The barber and his wife come, and the doctor with his third or fourth wife, and Prince and his Italian wife are always there. The father, laid up with a broken leg, busted head, split ribs, and ripped arm, teaches his son to play chess on a little folding set he has from college. The mother sits at the foot of the bed and watches. They all wait for the oil dealer to come. The oil dealer always brings a paper sack of cold beer and ice cream and silly jokes.

You ought to meet my cousin Ruth Ann, the oil dealer tells the mother. She's a lot of fun and she has a daughter they said ought to be tested, too.

The special child has never seen a movie before. He is stunned. *Misty of Chincoteague*, on a mile-high drive-in screen. In Ruth Ann's Rambler she drives fast down the middle of the highway, her and the mother in the front seat, the two special children in the backseat. Christie, the other special child, with impossibly tangled red hair, says, Actually, *Misty* is for babies. Christie says if the special child liked *Misty* so much then he ought to come over and watch *The Invisible Man* on TV on Saturday. She says she knows how to make the house dark even in the afternoon and make it scary. The special child is still hung over from concentrating on *Misty*. It was almost better than Moe throwing suitcases from the train. While he is thinking this, Christie says to her mother that she is going to vomit. Ruth Ann keeps her Rambler going fast down the middle of the highway talking a mile a minute to the mother and says for Christie just to do it out the window. Lean way out and try not to get any on the car.

The special child holds Christie's legs as she leans way out and vomits. It feels like she might crawl all the way out if he does not hold her. He wraps his arms around her legs and presses his face against her bottom. When she is through he pulls her in the window; her red hair is a solid mess of tangles. The special child helps clean her mouth and face of popcorn and 7-Up with an old black slip that for some reason is crumpled up on the floorboard of the backseat of Ruth Ann's rambling car.

When the father is feeling better and up on crutches he decides to drive them down to Louisiana and the mother packs that day even though they won't be leaving for a week or so. He says they will have a vacation, visit some battlefields on the way down, make a long trip out of it. He will borrow a car from the company, a gray sedan with a two-way radio in it.

Before they leave on their vacation, the school invites them to have the special child tested on the first Saturday after school closes for the summer. First grade is over. Bring good pencils.

When the special child shows up with the mother for the testing the mother is glad to see Ruth Ann there with Christie and Christie's cousin Lynn. They are all three going to be tested together. Most of the test is written and is fun, but some of the test is with a witch. The witch has cards and blocks and boxes of gears. Once during the testing, Christie has to vomit. Lynn doesn't even care that Christie has to vomit. Christie is always vomiting. That is one reason she is being tested.

The closer they get to Louisiana on their vacation, the madder the father gets. Maybe it is all the battlefields. Maybe it is all his broken places. Maybe it is all his land underwater. Maybe it is all the driving time he has to think about everything, driving on the roads before there are interstates between Virginia and Louisiana. Maybe it is going home. Maybe it is because everybody thought he would go real far in life and thinks he should be there now, him near the top of his class in chemical engineering at Rice, the people at NASA wanting him bad, and then in his senior year him switching to LSU and forestry so he could be out in the woods by himself all the time. Maybe that is underneath it all, riding in a hot car over asphalt and tar with a trembly wife and special son for days. Maybe he just doesn't like people at all, maybe that's it.

At the mother's mother's house in Louisiana, they have spicy chicken and rice and beer in coolers in the kitchen and black coffee and fried bread and brothers coming in off shifts in the oilfields and refineries to see their big sister, the brothers tossing the special child up in the air and taking him out back to see how they are putting a stock car together. Cousins and uncles and aunts come over all speaking French and Uncle Comille with his pigeons and Buddy with his five sons. Only the mother's father sits a little away from things at the table playing solitaire and smoking unfiltered cigarettes. In his life he has been a miner, a baker, a rigger, a cowboy, a pipefitter. To make ends meet, he now drives a mowing tractor at a golf course, bringing home buckets of old golf balls he runs over. Maybe now he is tired.

It is quiet across town at the father's mother's house. You can hear the grandfather clock on the back gallery ticking all through the house. Dinner will be at high noon. There are no brothers or sisters. One cousin, somewhere. Big Bill, the father's father, lets the special child, his only grandchild, sit in his lap and play with his Shriner's ring and with his warts. Before high-noon dinner of turkey and dumplings Big Bill has a shot glass on either arm of his chair, one filled with bourbon, the other with ice water. The special child likes the moments in between the drinks when the body he is slumped against relaxes and the warm deep breath blown out down on the top of his head smells sweet.

The father's mother is a big woman from Sumrall, Mississippi, who was used to more than her husband has provided over the years. He had been away a lot on Huey Long's Special Police force and then on the railroad, and when he came home he would go away on the weekends hunting and fishing with his best friend, a Jew, Dr. Goldsmith. The father's mother did not like Huey Long, and she does not like Jews. She had a pet Negro growing up named Scrap. When Big Bill takes their laundry in to the black part of town, he often stays all morning, listening and talking and eating fried-oyster po'boy sandwiches. Since Big Bill retired and came home for good, he mostly stays in his shop in the garage putting people's clocks together for them. The big clock at the nuns' convent is always stopping, and when he goes over there to fix it, they feed him lunch and make him stay all day.

On a side trip to New Orleans the women go shopping with the father along to watch their bags and Big Bill takes the special child to Jackson Square to feed the pigeons. It is hot and Big Bill takes the child to some bars off Bourbon Street to get out of the sun and to meet some friends of his from the old days. In the bars are friendly people with parrots on their shoulders, big laughing bartenders in white shirts and black bow ties who give Big Bill his two shot glasses and the child ginger ale colored with maraschino cherry juice. Big Bill lets the child sit on his lap on his bar stool while they watch the street go past the open barroom doors.

Up on a glass shelf in one of the bars they go into to get out of the sun that afternoon, the child sees a wind-up toy lit from underneath with green and red lights. The bartender takes it down and winds it up and sets it on the bar. A little monkey in a fez plays the drums nodding his head and kicking his feet. It is like Moe throwing luggage, like Misty swimming off Chincoteague: so long as that monkey keeps playing the drums and nodding his head and kicking his feet, time stands still for the special child. Wind it up again, wind it up, can we wind it up again please sir?

Come on Snort, Big Bill calls his grandson, and Big Bill takes them out of the bar and onto a streetcar out to Audubon Park. A lady in her bathrobe on the streetcar has a plastic flower in her hair and carries a long piece of wrought iron tipped like a spear it looks like she has pulled out of someone's fence. She asks Big Bill for a dime and he gives her a dollar. Where you going? she asks. I'm taking my grandson to the zoo. Well, say hello to my uncle, says the lady. He works at the zoo? asks Big Bill. He's locked up in the monkey house, says the lady. He's a monkey's uncle. Well, we'll say hello, says Big Bill, we're on our way to the monkey house. My boy here seems to like monkeys.

It's incredible, the monkey house. A big castle surrounded by a moat with millions of monkeys playing with themselves like humans and shouting at the tourists and sometimes flinging a handful of poo-poo at the people leaning over the rail.

I want to stay here all day, says the special child. OK, says Big Bill, we will, and they stay until it is time for them to go.

On their way out, the child sees a man walking around the monkey house. The man is picking up trash with a nail on the end of a stick. He carries a big burlap sack slung over his shoulder for the stuff he finds. He doesn't even have to bend over to pick it up because he has the nail on the end of the stick.

Is that that man's job? the child asks Big Bill.

Yes, says Big Bill, that's what he does.

He gets to walk around the monkey house all day with a nail on the end of a stick finding stuff? wonders the child.

Yes, says Big Bill.

In the storeroom off the back gallery of Big Bill's house the child finds lots of treasures. There are *National Geographics* from the very first year. The child mostly likes the castle, ship, and monkey issues. He finds his father's helmet from when his father was in the army. There is one thing he finds that he likes a lot better than the *National Geographics*: a box of old photographs of blown-apart people and horses and snow. When he pulls it out and asks about it, they take it away from him, and on his later visits the box of photographs is gone.

In the First World War, when Big Bill was a young man enlisted from deep within the bayous to fight the Germans, some officers took him into French towns with them because he spoke a kind of French, this kind of French being his first language, English an annoying clutterance later. The officers liked Big Bill and Big Bill became not only their interpreter but an ambassador of sorts, because Big Bill got along well with the French people they met and the French people liked Big Bill and made allowance for the coarser Americans, his army superiors.

As a gift, an officer had given Big Bill a simple box camera. With the simple box camera, Big Bill took dramatic photographs of his friends struggling and dying with their horse-drawn artillery in the heavy snows of the Argonne Forest. The only happy photograph was taken by a stranger on the returning troopship, showing a very thin Big Bill and two other soldiers, all who were left of the cannonade they had been.

Here's something you can play with, the grandmother tells the special child. She sets an old Royal typewriter on the dining-room table. Write me a letter, write me a story. The child tries to type the story of Misty of Chincoteague in several sentences. It takes most of the afternoon.

When it is time to go back to Virginia, the mother cries and begs to stay at her mother's house. Here, take some food I am making for you for the trip, the mother's mother says, ignoring her crying. The mother's mother cooks spicy food and fries up some bread and this makes the father angry because he hates when his clothes smell like fried bread. The child is afraid he will have to return to Virginia with his father by himself. They have a big going-away barbecue for the mother, and her brothers tie her up in the backyard and wash her hair for her with the hose until she says uncle. Everybody laughs except the father, who watches from the garage where the stock car and tools are, sipping beer. When the child tries to save the mother one of his uncles sets him on top of the garage roof and later makes him ride a pony.

Sometimes, on the ride back to Virginia, because the company gray sedan with the two-way radio looks like an unmarked police car, the father drives up behind people he thinks are driving too fast and flashes his lights and makes them pull over, then he speeds off. He stops doing this when in Georgia he accidentally pulls over an unmarked police car and the state trooper is very angry at the father. Later on, in North Carolina, the father seethes and speeds faster.

It had been so hot while they had been away in Louisiana that the candles the mother had stuck in the Chianti bottles were drooped over on the mantel.

There is a lot of mail. There is a letter from the invention company where the father has sent an invention. It is an invention for hooking up a device onto a kite string that can send things up to the kite and then release them so they can float to the ground. The father got the idea watching the special child trying to slingshot his Japanese parachutists as high as he could in the backyard. The father tried to explain the idea to his brothers-in-law in

Louisiana and they were polite about it but you could tell they didn't understand why anyone would want an invention like that, an invention that sounded, even to the special child as his father explained it, like something a little childish. Right on the spot, the brothers-in-law took some pipes and welded together a cannon that would shoot old golf balls about a hundred yards. You can take it back to Virginia with you, they told the child when they were leaving, giving him the cannon, and they said good luck to the father about his invention, even if they didn't understand it. When the father gets home from Louisiana, the invention company doesn't understand the invention and they don't want it, either.

In the mail are the test results. One test result says the mother is most likely pregnant again. The other test result says the child is eligible for a special school if the father can afford it.

The father goes down to check on his underwater property. While he and his family were away in Louisiana, the idiots at the dam finally adjusted the water levels on the lake just right. The shoreline is exactly where he and the German predicted it would be. In the lowering fluctuations of the lake, all the German's beautiful sand has washed along the father's shoreline and blanketed his property with long, broad beaches. Where the German's beautiful beaches had been were ugly slick stretches of slippery red clay corrupted through and through by the black roots of drowned trees. Dat iz in der past, you must let it go, the father tells the angry German, and the German and his family move away.

In the fall the special child starts second grade. His second-grade teacher is Miss Caroon. Miss Caroon has seen his test results, so she lets him spend as much time as he wants reading *The Box Car Children* and Mark Twain in the cloakroom while the other children struggle with Dick and Jane and Baby and Spot. Miss Caroon lets him wear his father's army helmet in the classroom if he wants to, and she lets him try to pass off the wad of Confederate money he always carries. At Thanksgiving when he draws the Pilgrims coming to the New World in a Chinese junk greeted by Indians selling Live Bait and Cold Beer, she hangs his picture on the wall with all the rest without extraordinary commentary.

Miss Caroon gives the children in her class a list of words from which to make a story. In the stories the class turns in, dogs get up on the furniture when they aren't supposed to, or someone finds a coin. From the special child she receives "The Ancient Castle," in which a Good King goes away to conquer an enemy and while he is gone an Evil King comes and lays siege to the Good King's castle. The Evil King's men scale the walls and some of the Good King's favorite men are shot full of arrows and beheaded. Just when all seems to be lost, everyone looks up and sees a brilliant flash of light on a distant hill. It is the sun shining off the Good King's shield. The Good King and his men come and slaughter the Evil King and all of the Evil King's men. The people in the Good King's castle are so happy they have a huge banquet and feast on roast duck and turkey. After they have eaten all they can eat, they begin singing the Good King's favorite songs. Miss Caroon reads the child's story out loud to the class. She especially likes the last sentence in the story, and takes her time sounding it out: "And the singing went on for days."

Miss Caroon hands back the stories and the child receives an A-minus because he misspells *Ancient* in the title. This is a very good story, she tells the child. When his mother comes to visit on Parents' Day Miss Caroon tells her that her son is a special child, that he could be a writer someday if he wanted to be one. The mother shakes her head sadly and tells Miss Caroon the truth. She has to tell Miss Caroon that all the child wants to be when he grows up is the man who walks around the monkey house all day with a nail on the end of a stick.

Notes on Contributors

Rick Bass is the author of eleven books of fiction and nonfiction, including *The Watch*, *Oil Notes*, *Winter*, *The Ninemile Wolves*, *The Book of Yaak*, and most recently, *The Sky, the Stars, and the Wilderness*. A new novel, *Where the Sea Used to Be*, will be published soon. He grew up in Texas and now lives with his family on a remote ranch in Montana.

Tom Chiarella teaches English at Depaux in Greencastle, Indiana. Alfred A. Knopf published his collection of stories, *Foley's Luck*. His textbook on writing dialogue (*Writing Dialogue*, first published by Writer's Digest Books in 1996) has just been issued by Story Press.

Pat Conroy is the author of *Beach Music*, *The Prince of Tides*, *The Great Santini*, *The Lords of Discipline*, and *The Water Is Wide*. He graduated from the Citadel in 1967.

Margaret F. M. Davis was born in Mount Vernon, New York. A lifelong New Yorker with an avid interest in literature, she lives and farms part-time in Virginia.

Richard Ford won the Pulitzer Prize for his fifth novel, *Independence Day*. He is also the author of *A Piece of My Heart*, *The Ultimate Good Luck*, *The Sportswriter*, and *Wildlife*, as well as a story collection, *Rock Springs*, and three novellas collectively entitled *Women with Men*.

MARY GAITSKILL grew up outside of Detroit. She is the author of the collections *Bad Behavior* and *Because They Wanted To* and the novel *Two Girls, Fat and Thin*.

ELIZABETH GILBERT has published a collection of stories entitled *Pilgrims*. Her fiction has appeared in *Esquire, Story*, the *Paris Review, GQ, Ploughshares*, and the *Mississippi Review*. In 1996 she was awarded the New Discovery Prize. A contributing writer to *GQ*, she lives with her husband in New York City.

BARRY HANNAH lives in Oxford, Mississippi. He is the author of many works of fiction, including *Geronimo Rex, The Nightwatchmen, Airships, Ray, The Tennis Handsome, Captain Maximus, Bats out of Hell*, and, most recently, the story collection *High Lonesome*. He has been honored by the American Academy of Arts and Letters for his achievement in fiction.

JIM HARRISON is a poet and a novelist whose books include *After Ikkyu and Other Poems, Julip, The Woman Lit by Fireflies, Dalva, Legends of the Fall, Farmer, Selected and New Poems, The Theory and Practice of Rivers*, and *Wolf*. He lives with his family on a farm in northern Michigan.

AMY HEMPEL teaches in the Graduate Writing Program at Bennington College. Her most recent book is *Tumble Home*, a novella and stories. She is also the author of *Reasons to Live* and *At the Gates of the Animal Kingdom*. Her work has appeared in *Harper's, Vanity Fair*, and *The Quarterly*.

MARK JACOBSON has published two novels, most recently *Everyone and No One* (Villard). His first novel, *Gojiro*, was published in 1991. He has been a staff writer and contributing editor at *New York* magazine, the *Village Voice, Rolling Stone, Natural History*, and *Esquire*. He lives with his family in Brooklyn.

DARIUS JAMES is the author of *Negrophobia* and *That's Blaxploitation!*, both published by St. Martin's Press. He lives in Brooklyn.

DENIS JOHNSON is a poet and fiction writer living in northern Idaho. His works include the collection *Jesus' Son* and the novels *Already Dead, Resuscitation of a Hanged Man, The Stars at Noon, Fiskadoro*, and *Angels*. His several volumes of poetry have been collected in *The Throne of the Third Heaven of the Nations Millennium General Assembly*.

THOM JONES attended and taught at the Iowa Writers' Workshop. He is the author of the collections *Cold Snap* and *The Pugilist at Rest*, which was nominated for the National Book Award. His stories have appeared in *Esquire, Harper's,* the *New Yorker,* and other magazines. He lives in the state of Washington.

NORMAN MAILER was born in 1923 in Long Branch, New Jersey, and grew up in Brooklyn, New York. He published his first novel, *The Naked and the Dead,* in 1948. He won the National Book Award and the Pulitzer Prize in 1968 for *Armies of the Night,* and was awarded the Pulitzer Prize again in 1980 for *The Executioner's Song*. His most recent book is *The Time of Our Time*.

TERRY MCMILLAN is the author of *Mama, Disappearing Acts, Waiting to Exhale,* and *How Stella Got Her Groove Back*. She also edited *Breaking Ice: An Anthology of Contemporary African-American Fiction*.

RICK MOODY grew up in Connecticut and now lives in Brooklyn. His most recent novel is *Purple America*. His works also include *The Ice Storm, Garden State,* and *The Ring of Brightest Angels Around Heaven,* the title story of which won the *Paris Review*'s Aga Khan Prize. He is the coeditor, with Darcey Steinke, of *Joyful Noise: The New Testament Revisited*. His fiction and essays have appeared in *Esquire,* the *New Yorker, Harper's,* and *Grand Street*.

ANN PATCHETT is the author of three novels, *The Magician's Assistant, Taft,* and *The Patron Saint of Liars*. She is originally from Los Angeles and now lives in Nashville.

JAYNE ANNE PHILLIPS has published two novels, *Machine Dreams* and *Shelter,* and a number of short-story collections, including *Counting, Sweethearts, Fast Lanes,* and *Black Tickets,* the last of which was nominated for a National Book Critics Circle Award. She grew up in West Virginia.

MARK RICHARD received the PEN/Ernest Hemingway Award for best first work of fiction for his collection *The Ice at the Bottom of the*

World. He is also the author of *Fishboy*. His stories have been published in *Shenandoah, Harper's, Esquire,* and the *New Yorker*. He was born in Louisiana and raised in Texas and Virginia.

JAMES SALTER is the author of *A Sport and a Pastime*, now published by Modern Library. His other works of fiction include *Light Years, The Hunters, Solo Faces, The Arm of Flesh,* and *Dusk and Other Stories,* which won the PEN/Faulkner Award. His most recent book is the memoir *Burning the Days.*

LEE SMITH grew up in the mountains of Virginia and lives now in North Carolina. She has published nine novels, including *Oral History, Fair and Tender Ladies, The Devil's Dream,* and *Black Mountain Breakdown*. She is also the author of three short-story collections: *Cakewalk, Me and My Baby View the Eclipse,* and, most recently, *News of the Spirit.*

ROBERT STONE has just published his sixth novel, *Damascus Gate*. His first, *A Hall of Mirrors*, won a William Faulkner Foundation Award. *Dog Soldiers* received a National Book Award. He is also the author of *A Flag for Sunrise, Children of Light,* and *Outerbridge Reach*. His first collection of stories, *Bear and His Daughter*, came out in 1997. He lives with his wife in Connecticut and travels widely.

WILLIAM VOLLMANN recently completed a book about the nature of violence. His works of fiction include *You Bright and Risen Angels, The Rainbow Stories, The Atlas,* and three volumes of his "Seven Dreams" series: *The Ice-Shirt, Fathers and Crows,* and *The Rifles*. He makes his home in California.

DAVID FOSTER WALLACE is the author of the novels *Infinite Jest* and *The Broom of the System*. He has also published a collection of essays, *A Supposedly Fun Thing I'll Never Do Again*, and a volume of short stories, *Girl with Curious Hair*. The recipient of a MacArthur fellowship, he lives in Bloomington, Illinois.

JOY WILLIAMS's novels and short-story collections include *State of Grace*, which was nominated for a National Book Award, as well as *The Changeling, Breaking and Entering, Taking Care,* and *Escapes*. Her stories and essays have appeared in *Esquire,* the *New Yorker,*

Harper's, and the *Paris Review*. She is a recipient of the Mildred and Harold Strauss Living Award for her fiction.

STEPHEN WRIGHT is the author of three novels, *Going Native, M31: A Family Romance*, and *Meditations in Green*. He lives in New York City.